DESSERTS
AND
PASTRIES

Over two hundred and fifty recipes
collected by
LEONE BOSI

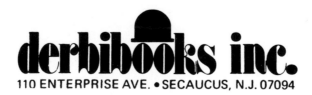
derbibooks inc.
110 ENTERPRISE AVE. • SECAUCUS, N.J. 07094

© 1972 Arnoldo Mondadori Editore, Milano
All Rights Reserved

© 1974 English Translation
Lutterworth Press, Guildford and London

Library of Congress 74-82432
ISBN 0-89009-012-2

Printed and Bound in Italy 'by
A. Mondadori Editore - Verona

CONTENTS

EDITOR'S NOTE

The lists of ingredients do not include butter or fat used for greasing, or flour, sugar and breadcrumbs for preparing tins. All references to flour and sugar indicate plain flour and granulated sugar, unless otherwise stated.

The following may be taken as general guidelines for the oven temperatures (they are given in Fahrenheit, for an electric oven):

hot———— 375°—450°
moderate——325°—350°
cool———— 275°—300°

Where wafers are required, continental-type cookie wafers are called for. These should be available from a good delicatessen, in various sizes.

INTRODUCTION

This book presents a collection of recipes which include traditional Italian dishes, famous desserts from other countries and others from the so-called "international cuisine".

The influence of industrial confectionery has made itself felt above all in the use of kitchen implements: gone almost are the mortars, sieves—from flat ones to the conical *chinois*—, collections of spoons and ladles; there are fewer picturesque copper molds, *savarin* molds, rabbit- or lobster-shaped molds. Today it is quicker and more practical to serve most dishes—from *zuppa inglese* to fruit salads—in salad bowls, and certainly there is no call to decorate them elaborately.

As far as molds are concerned, the following should be sufficient:

    2 round, smooth-sided cake pans (one of 9 in. in diameter and one of 12 in.), preferably with a spring clip

    1 rectangular cake pan for plum cakes

    1 *charlotte* mold (domed, with a round *embouchure*, about $2\frac{1}{2}$ pints in capacity).

It is important also to have:

    1 fine-meshed strainer for creams.

The following electrical implements, practically indispensable to the younger pastry-cook, were totally unknown to our grandmothers:

    1 electric mixer with accessory for whipping (and mayonnaise)

    1 electric grinder, for almonds, hazelnuts, etc.

    1 electric handmixer (if the mixer is too small).

Amongst the less important items, apart from scales (which, hopefully, are also used for other, non-sweet dishes), we recommend a measuring cup for liquids, a rubber spatula for clearing up cream from the bottom and sides of dishes, a pastry brush, a ravioli wheel with serrated edge and a forcing bag for fillings and decoration.

As far as the ingredients themselves are concerned:

—Leavening can be obtained, according to the type of pastry one is making, with fresh yeast bought from a baker's, or else with ready-made mixtures. This should be determined by personal experience and the attitude of one's table companions.

—It is possible to buy pastry mix: all one has to do then is to follow the instructions on the package for working the dough and baking it. Here too the use of these substitutes has to be determined by personal preference. In the matter of fats (for shortcrust Artusi recommends using lard but hardly anyone uses that nowadays) this also applies.

—Although there exist small ice-cream containers for use in the freezer, the recipes in this book refer to ready-made ice-creams (found in supermarkets in various sizes and shapes) to be elaborated upon as little as possible.

—As has already been mentioned, small items of confectionary and decoration may be bought ready-made (the *choux* used in the St Honoré for instance). But the creams and fillings to be piped through a forcing bag must be home-made. The same may be said of *vol-au-vent* cases, meringues, profiteroles, *cannoli* (Sicilian pastry filled with cream), etc. Some of the recipes in this book are more complicated than others, especially those in the chapter called *Special Occasions*; nevertheless they can be made successfully with time. In every case the decoration has been kept to a minimum. We have abstained from referring to the prestigious examples of soft sculpture which once were— and still are—the pride of chefs capable of creating wonders of architectural confectionery, sugar flowers, butter statuettes, after models which—a case unique in the history of decorative arts—stopped at about 1880. It would have been very easy to reproduce in this book the famous designs of Carême, the Prince of Benevento's chef; of Gouffé; or of Antonio Vialardi, assistant chef of Victor Emmanuel II. But, as we have said, today's reality is different.

It is possible to make marvellous desserts without undue work at the stove and with just a cream-filled forcing bag in one's hand.

BASIC RECIPES

Pancake Batter

Mix the flour, egg and milk together in a bowl; then add the butter (melted), brandy and pinch of salt and flavor to taste with a spoonful of orange-flower water. Leave to stand for at least one hour and strain before using to make your pancakes. By using the same spoon or ladle each time to pour the batter into the pan you can be sure of even-sized pancakes. To cook them properly you need a frying pan which is exactly the same diameter as the size of pancake you require and it should be lightly buttered first. The pancake should be turned out as soon as it is evenly colored on both sides.

2 cups flour	2½ tablespoons brandy
3 eggs	pinch of salt
1 pint milk	orange-flower water
knob of butter	

Choux Paste

In a saucepan mix the water, the sugar, butter and salt. Heat until just boiling. Take off the stove and pour in the flour, beating strongly: still beating, return to the heat and cook until the paste no longer runs off the spoon.

Remove from the heat again and add the eggs two by two, mixing them well in. When the paste is quite smooth flavor with a little orange-flower water.

1 pint water	1 cup flour
½ cup sugar	8 eggs
¾ cup butter	orange-flower water
1 teaspoon salt	

Shortcrust Pastry

Mostly used for tarts and pies, particularly fruit tarts, although it naturally has many other uses and always gives good results.

Mix the flour with a pinch of salt and make a well in the center. Put the butter, egg yolks, sugar and grated lemon peel into the well. Working fast and lightly with a balloon whisk beat the ingredients well together adding water, little by little, until you have a smooth, elastic dough. Form into a ball; dust with flour and leave to stand, covered with a cloth or a bowl, for at least 40 minutes before use.

3 cups flour	4 egg yolks
pinch of salt	$\frac{1}{2}$ cup sugar
$\frac{3}{4}$ cup butter	grated lemon peel

Puff Pastry

Mix the flour with a good pinch of salt in a bowl then add a little water and mix, first with a wooden spoon, then by hand, until you have a smooth ball of dough. Dust your working top with flour, roll out the dough to a rectangle about $\frac{1}{4}$ in. thick. Arrange the butter, divided into little pieces, on the center section of the dough (the butter should be the same consistency as the dough, not too hard or too soft). Fold the dough up over the butter as though you were wrapping a package. Roll out with the rolling pin again; this time getting the dough longer and slightly more stretched.

This next part of the operation is the most delicate, as care must be taken that the butter becomes spread evenly on both sides of the dough: now fold the dough over itself three times (like an envelope) give a light turn with the rolling pin so the top flap is flattened into the rest. Leave to stand for 20 minutes then roll out again. Repeat this last folding and rolling (dusting the rolling pin with flour each time) once more. Leave to stand again and repeat this operation six times. This is the only way to get light puff pastry.

"Half-puff" pastry is made more quickly: make as above but giving three turns instead of six and leaving to stand for only 15 minutes between turns. If you have the time, full puff pastry always gives the best results.

The uses of puff pastry are innumerable e.g. as part of, or to serve, with all kinds of desserts, salads etc. . . . This is undoubtedly the aristocrat of pastries.

$2\frac{1}{2}$ cups flour	1 pint water
pinch of salt	$\frac{3}{4}$ cup butter

Pâte Brisé

This pastry is an alternative to shortcrust and may be used for all kinds of tarts and pies. In making tarts and pies whether you use shortcrust or *pâte brisé* is a matter of personal taste or convenience and your own capabilities, rather than any culinary rule. . . . For instance a strawberry tart will be just as good made with shortcrust or *pâte brisé*.
Make a well in the center of the flour, tip in the butter, sugar and salt. Add the water and mix the whole well together working fast. *Pâte brisé* should not, in fact, be too smooth. Form the dough into a ball; cover with a cloth and leave to stand for at least six hours before use.

2 cups flour	*pinch of salt*
½ cup butter	*½ cup water*
¾ cup sugar	

Pasta Margherita

Beat the eggs in a saucepan, add the sugar and over a moderate heat, mix or beat rapidly until the mixture has obviously increased in volume. Remove from the heat, stir a little more and add first the flour, then the butter (previously melted and left to cool). Gently beat the whole together for a long time, then pour into a buttered and floured pan (or better still, one lined with buttered paper). Cook in a moderate oven for about 40 minutes.

6 eggs	*2 cups flour*
1 cup sugar	*1 cup butter*

Pan di Spagna (Spanish Bread)

Pan di spagna is the invaluable base for all kinds of cream tarts and pastries. It is useful when making it to make enough for several usages, as it keeps very well in the refrigerator.

Break the eggs into a saucepan and add the sugar, grated lemon peel and pinch of salt. Heat in a bain-marie, continually whisking until the mixture augments in volume.

Remove from the heat and pour in the previously mixed flour and potato starch; then, still beating, add the melted butter. Work well until you have a smooth paste which can then be poured into a rather wide, floured and buttered pie plate. Put into a moderate-to-cool oven and leave to cook for at least 40 minutes, then take out. Leave the *Pan di spagna* until quite cold before using to make your dessert. If you want it to keep, remember to store it wrapped in tinfoil in the refrigerator.

8 eggs	*1 cup flour*
1 cup sugar	*$\frac{3}{4}$ cup potato starch*
grated lemon peel	*1 tablespoon butter*
pinch of salt	

Genoese Pastry

This is a firm sponge-cake type of pastry used for pies, trifles and gâteau-type desserts *(Translator's Note)*.

This pastry requires time and attention but these are more than justified by the results. With this pastry many kinds of desserts may be made and it can be used as an alternative base for various recipes.

Put the whole eggs, with the sugar, into a pan which will go in a bain-marie and will heat easily. Beat the mixture well, gradually beating faster and faster. Take care the mixture heats without cooking. Lower the heat as necessary. When the paste has doubled in volume and becomes lighter so that it runs from the beater remove the pan from the bain-marie and continue to beat evenly until it goes cold. At this point it may be flavored with a spoonful of the liqueur of your choice or grated lemon peel.

When the paste is cool add the softened butter and the flour, continuing to beat evenly until it is homogeneous but not too smooth. Butter the tin or baking pan you want to use (don't use an aluminium pan or your pastry will turn a terrible greyish color) and pour in the paste, put into a moderate oven and cook for 30–40 minutes.

Genoese pastry is cooked when it is evenly golden brown all over and springs back from the pressure of your fingers.

6 eggs	*$\frac{1}{2}$ cup butter*
1 cup sugar	*$1\frac{1}{4}$ cups flour*
grated lemon peel or	
liqueur for flavoring	

Crême Anglaise

As is the case with so many recipes "English cream" is known by its French name (*Translator's Note*).
Pour the milk into a saucepan, bring to the boil and remove from the heat. Add the vanilla and leave to stand for a few minutes.
Meanwhile beat the egg yolks hard with the sugar and, when they are fluffy and well puffed up, mix in the milk. Return to the heat, still stirring until mixture thickens. Turn off the heat and continue to mix for a few minutes.

1¼ cups milk	4 egg yolks
3 drops vanilla essence	½ cup sugar

Pastry Cream *(Crème Pâtissière)*

Beat the egg yolks in a saucepan with the sugar to a firm snow. Add the flour little by little and flavor with a pinch of salt. Continue to beat lightly but now over a moderate heat gradually adding the previously boiled milk flavored with vanilla. Continue to stir until the cream thickens. Leave for a few minutes then remove from heat and leave to go cold, before using.

6 egg yolks	pinch of salt
1 cup sugar	2¼ cups milk
½ cup flour	pinch of vanilla

Starch Cream

Beat the egg yolks and sugar in a saucepan, continuing to beat until the mixture is fairly firm. Now add the starch dissolved in a little milk and then, still beating, add the milk, vanilla and lemon peel. Cook over a moderate heat, continuing to stir, until the mixture is resistant to the spoon.

4 egg yolks	2¼ cups milk
¾ cup sugar	1 envelope vanilla powder
½ cup starch	lemon peel

An example of fruit salad made more fascinating by a decoration of whipped cream.

Chocolate Cream

This cream is made like the pastry cream just described. But when the milk and vanilla boils, the chocolate is melted in it; the remainder of the operation is carried out as before.

6 egg yolks	*2¼ cups milk*
1 cup sugar	*pinch of vanilla*
½ cup flour	*1 cup grated baking chocolate*

Crème St Honoré

A variation of the pastry cream already described. When the pastry cream is removed from the heat, 7 egg whites, well beaten to a firm snow, are added.
Crème St Honoré should be used immediately. If it has to be left to wait it is best to add gelatine in the ratio of 2 leaves to each pint of cream.

6 egg yolks	*pinch of vanilla*
1 cup sugar	*7 egg whites*
½ cup flour	*leaf gelatine*
2¼ cups milk	

Chantilly Cream

Whipped cream is of basic importance in pastry making. It can be used in practically all desserts, either as flavoring or decoration. Modern technology has put at our disposal the means of making it in a moment: all you need is an electric mixer and fresh cream to make whipped cream without any effort. Naturally, whipped cream, as we shall see in the recipe, can be made by hand with an egg beater but a mixer is without doubt essential in any well-equipped kitchen. However here is the recipe for Chantilly, or sweet whipped, cream. Chill the cream in the refrigerator for a few hours until really cold. Pour into a bowl and beat with an egg beater, slowly at first and then gradually faster. Stop when the cream is well fluffed up but still elastic. Now add the sugar, gently folding it in.

To prepare the cream just before serving is undoubtedly best. It can, however, be kept for a limited period in the refrigerator (under cover so it does not absorb other food flavors) on the coldest shelf.

2½ cups fresh cream	½ cup caster sugar

Strawberry Cream

Wash and pick over strawberries; put them into a bowl and cover them with warm sugar syrup flavored with vanilla. Leave to go cold and then pass through a fine sieve. This makes another cream for filling or covering desserts.

¾ lb fresh strawberries	vanilla flavoring
1½ cups sugar syrup (described on page 27)	

Frangipani Cream

Boil the milk with the vanilla. In a separate saucepan, beat the eggs and egg yolks with the sugar. When firm and well fluffed up flavor with salt and add the flour, mixing well in. Put onto the heat and then, still beating, add the milk little by little. Leave to cook for a few minutes, then remove from heat. Now add the crumbled plain cookies and butter, working it well so that it is all mixed in smoothly. Pour into a mold or dish, or onto the dessert being made, and then chill well in the refrigerator.

2½ cups milk	pinch of salt
1 teaspoon vanilla powder	1 cup flour
2 eggs	4 dry cookies or macaroons
3 egg yolks	2 tablespoons butter
½ cup sugar	

Zabaione

Beat the eggs with the sugar in a saucepan until fluffy; little by little work in the marsala—
about the equivalent of 12 half-eggshells full.
Cook in a bain-marie stirring constantly. The Zabaione is ready when it begins to thicken
and increase in volume.

6 eggs   *dry marsala*
¾ cup sugar

**Opposite: chocolate topping is widely used in
ornate cake making.**

Below: a bavarois covered with Zabaione.

Chocolate Topping

Break up the chocolate into a small saucepan, heat over a bain-marie. Stir continuously taking care that not a drop of water gets into the pan. If this happens the melting chocolate will separate and remain so.
When the chocolate is well melted and looks smooth remove from the heat and pour over dessert immediately.

chocolate couverture as required

Caramel

Pour the sugar into a small saucepan adding enough cold water just to moisten it. Stirring well, cook until sugar turns brown. Add the warm water, still stirring, and leave to cook until the sugar is quite dissolved. Strain and use immediately or keep in a hermetically sealed jar.

½ cup sugar *cold water*	*about ½ cup warm water*

Icing

Icing or glazing of one kind or another is of basic importance in pâtisserie. It is used to cover all kinds of tarts, pastries, desserts, cakes etc. . . . Making icing is not difficult; what is more complicated is spreading it evenly over a surface. To spread it easily use a lightly oiled spatula so that the finished work is smooth and shining.

Sugar Icing

Melt the powdered sugar with a little water in a pan. Flavor it with orange-flower water or any liqueur of your choice. The consistency should be thick and it should be spread while still warm.
Alternatively you can color icing by using any proprietary brand of coloring essence.

powdered sugar *water or lemon juice*	*flavoring or coloring*

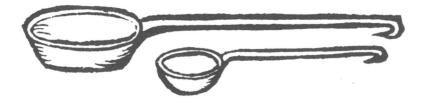

Coffee Icing

Melt the powdered sugar with good concentrated coffee over heat. Spread it whilst still warm.

powdered sugar	*strong coffee*

Chocolate Icing

Grate the chocolate couverture into a saucepan adding a few spoonfuls of sugar syrup (according to quantity desired) and a little powdered sugar. Melt the whole in a bain-marie and use immediately.

chocolate couverture	*powdered sugar*
sugar syrup (described overleaf)	

Water Icing

Dissolve the powdered sugar in a little water and flavor with whatever liqueur you prefer. Maraschino is good.

powdered sugar	*liqueur*

Various icing examples.

Royal Icing

Royal icing is extremely simple to make: just mix the powdered sugar with egg whites to get a good paste consistency. This kind of icing must be used immediately as it hardens very fast.

powdered sugar	egg whites

Sugar Syrup

Pour the water over the sugar in a saucepan. Mix well and bring to the boil. Remove from heat and skim. Return to the boil again for a few minutes and then take off the heat for good. Flavor to taste with a small glass of liqueur of your choice.

This kind of sugar syrup is used in various types of desserts, mostly for moistening and lining pastry bases or to finish off dessert pastries.

1 cup sugar	liqueur for flavoring
$\frac{3}{4}$ cup water	

Praline

For the best results you need a good copper pan. Failing this the recipe will work with a stainless steel one, which by the nature of the metal does not impart any taste to your food. Pour the sugar into the pan over a low heat and stir continuously. When the sugar begins to turn a light brown in color add the almonds, previously soaked in cold water. Tip the pan up leaving only a corner over the heat, and, working with a wooden spoon, stir and scrape well until the sugar turns dark gold.

Remove pan from the heat and pour contents out onto a previously oiled marble slab. Spread out, about $\frac{1}{3}$ in. thick, and score the surface with a knife so as to mark out small rectangular divisions.

When completely cold break up into small pieces, using the marked-out lines.

$1\frac{1}{4}$ cups sugar	$1\frac{1}{4}$ cups peeled almonds

Nougat

Pour the honey into a saucepan and heat over a moderate flame without boiling. Whip egg whites to a firm snow and delicately mix in. Meanwhile melt the sugar over a moderate heat in a separate saucepan. When quite melted add the honey and egg white mixture stirring for a few minutes, then remove from heat.

Now add the previously peeled and browned almonds, still stirring. Line nougat moulds, or similar, with the rice paper and pour in the mixture so that each mould is filled to the top, smoothing with a spatula; cover with more rice paper and put a heavy weight on top. The nougat will be ready to eat the following day.

1 cup honey	1¾ cups almonds
2 egg whites	rice paper
1¼ cups sugar	

Butter Cream

Butter cream is used mainly for filling sponge layer cakes or for flans or other cold desserts. You must of course choose the freshest and best quality butter.

Work the butter in a bowl with a spatula. When it is well softened add the caster sugar, still mixing hard. When the butter cream is ready you can add flavoring of your choice: liqueur, pinch of vanilla, orange or lemon juice or cocoa.

$\frac{3}{4}$ cup butter	$\frac{1}{2}$ cup caster sugar

Almond Paste (Italian Style)

Scald the almonds in boiling water, then peel them. Using a pestle and mortar crush them finely with the vanilla-flavored sugar. (Instead of vanilla sugar you can use a liqueur of your choice, such as Kirsch, brandy, rum, Maraschino etc. . . .)

When the almonds are well ground up and reduced to a paste put into a bowl and, mixing hard, add the sugar which should first be melted to the dark golden stage.

The almond paste is now ready and can be used either as filling or topping for any number of pastries and desserts.

1 cup almonds	1 cup granulated sugar
1 teaspoon sugar flavored with vanilla	

Honey Almond Paste

Crush the almonds finely, reduce to a paste, then add the caster sugar, vanilla-flavored sugar and honey. Mix well and hard so that all the ingredients are properly incorporated.

1 cup almonds	4 teaspoons vanilla-flavored sugar
2 cups caster sugar	2 tablespoons honey

Grape Juice Syrup

The Italians call this "cooked wine" and use it in pastry or dessert making as you would use fruit juice, jam or glaze *(Translator's Note)*.

Ideally this should be made from barely bruised grapes of the first must. But, given the difficulty of finding these, it will be all right if made from any ordinary grapes as follows. Remove the pits; wash the grapes well and then crush them. Filter the resulting juice through a muslin or fine sieve and then cook over a moderate heat in a stainless steel saucepan.

The cooking must continue for several hours. Stir from time to time. The syrup is ready when the mixture thickens and will hang on the spoon.

It may be kept in hermetically sealed glass jars or bottled.

White or red grapes of any kind

Basic Rice Condé

This is the classic way of cooking rice which is to be used as the basis of desserts or pastries, both hot and cold.

Boil up the milk and remove from the heat. Add the vanilla pods and leave, covered, to infuse for at least 15 minutes. Take out the vanilla pods and add the sugar, salt and butter. In a separate pan, cook the rice in water. When it has boiled wait for a minute, then drain the rice and pour it into the milk mixture adding the lemon peel. Return to the heat, bring to the boil, then lower the heat and leave to cook, covered, for about 25 minutes. Do not under any circumstances stir the rice during this period.

Remove from heat and carefully mix in the egg yolks.

2¼ cups milk	*1 tablespoon butter*
2 vanilla pods	*¾ cup rice*
2½ tablespoons sugar	*lemon peel*
pinch of salt	*3 egg yolks*

Meringues

Beat the egg whites to a firm snow then fold in the sugar—pouring it all in in one go. Work very carefully. Butter a baking sheet and arrange spoonfuls of the mixture on it sufficiently far apart to allow them room to cook without sticking together. Cook in a moderate oven for a few minutes, long enough to dry them out. Cooking time varies with the size of meringues but they are done when hard to the touch.

5 egg whites	1 cup sugar

Whipped cream can make a delicate icing.

THROUGHOUT THE DAY

A variation of the Torta Paradiso,
iced and decorated.

Breakfast

Crisp Cookies

Mix the flour, egg and softened butter to a paste with the sugar, cinnamon, clove, nutmeg and white pepper.

Work it all in for a few minutes, then leave to stand for a couple of hours. At the end of this time put the mixture into an icing bag with a vegetable rose nozzle. Squeeze out fingers of dough onto a buttered and floured cookie sheet. They should be about 4 in. long, leaving a reasonable space between each one. Cook in a moderate oven for about 10 minutes.

$2\frac{1}{4}$ cups flour	pinch of powdered clove
2 eggs	pinch of cinnamon
$\frac{3}{4}$ cup butter	pinch of white pepper
$\frac{1}{2}$ cup sugar	pinch of nutmeg

Pan Dolce

Literally "Sweet Bread", this is a kind of large fruity Italian Brioche *(Translator's Note)*. Dissolve the yeast in a little warm water and then mix to a paste with 3 tablespoons of the flour. Shape into a bun, cover and leave to prove in a warm place for at least 12 hours. Mix the risen yeast bun with the remaining flour, adding the butter, sugar, roughly chopped candied peel and the sultanas previously softened in water and well dried. Season with a pinch of salt. Mix well together until you have a smooth, homogeneous dough. Leave to rise again for about 4 hours. Shape into a big round loaf, then place on a buttered and floured metal cookie sheet. Cut a deep cross on the top and put into a moderate oven. It should cook for over an hour and is done when a knitting needle inserted into it will come out clean.

1 lb flour	$\frac{3}{4}$ cup mixed candied peel
$\frac{3}{4}$ packet yeast	$\frac{1}{2}$ cup sultanas
$\frac{1}{2}$ cup butter	salt
$\frac{1}{2}$ cup sugar	

Torta Paradiso

A classic Italian cake served plain at breakfast or may be iced for other meals *(Translator's Note)*.

Work the butter by hand until softened, but not too soft. Mix in the sugar, eggs and egg yolk, then, working with a wooden spoon, add ½ tablespoon of cornstarch and the grated lemon peel. Continue to mix for a few minutes. Little by little smoothly mix in the flour and remaining cornstarch. Take care that all is well mixed together.

Turn the whole into a baking pan which has been buttered and floured and leave to cook in a moderate oven until a knitting needle inserted into the cake will come out clean.

The cake should be cut cold and well dusted with caster sugar.

1 cup butter	*1¼ cups self-raising flour*
1 cup sugar	*4 whole eggs + 1 egg yolk*
1¼ cups cornstarch	*caster sugar*
grated peel of ½ lemon	

Simple Bun Ring

Mix the sugar and butter until fluffy. Add the egg yolks, flour and potato starch mixed together, the grated lemon peel and finally the yeast dissolved in a little warm water. Mix for a few minutes, then carefully fold in the egg whites which should have been beaten to a firm snow.

Pour this mixture into a buttered and floured baking mold and cook in a moderate oven for about 45 minutes.

½ cup sugar	*1¼ cups potato starch*
½ cup butter	*grated peel of 1 lemon*
3 eggs (separated)	*1 envelope dried yeast*
1¾ cups flour	

Granny's Bun Ring

Add the sugar, grated lemon peel and pinch of salt to the flour and mix well. Then add the eggs, softened butter, finely chopped bacon and the bicarbonate of soda diluted in a little milk. Mix vigorously to a smooth paste adding the remaining milk little by little and the marsala: then incorporate the bread dough which should be already risen.

Mix and knead vigorously for quite a long time until the dough is really smooth and homogeneous; arrange in a prepared ring mold, then leave, covered with a towel, to rise in a warm place for over an hour. Glaze with beaten egg and put into a hot oven to cook for about 45 minutes. Do not cut until cold.

3½ cups flour	*½ tablespoon bacon*
½ cup sugar	*pinch of bicarbonate of soda*
grated lemon peel	*¾ cup milk*
pinch of salt	*¼ cup marsala*
2 eggs	*2 oz bread dough*
1½ tablespoons butter	

Focaccia

Mix the flour with the yeast which has been dissolved in a little warm water, gradually adding more warm water until you have a smooth elastic dough. Form into a ball, then, having put it into a bowl and covered it with a towel, leave in a warm place to rise until it has doubled in volume.

Then add the pinch of salt, sugar, eggs, grated orange peel and the lard. Work in vigorously until the mixture no longer sticks to your fingers.

Grease a baking pan and arrange the dough on it about ¾ in. thick. Cover again with a towel and leave to rise again in a warm place for about 2 hours; then put into a hot oven and cook for not more than 30 minutes.

Focaccia is served cold, dusted with sugar. Thanks to its plain wholesome quality Focaccia can be eaten at any time of day.

3 cups flour	*2 eggs*
½ packet yeast	*grated orange peel*
pinch of salt	*½ cup lard*
½ cup caster sugar	*sugar for dusting*

Grape Bread

Work the bread dough with a third of the measured quantity of flour, a pinch of salt, 2 spoonfuls of oil and 1 egg. Then form into a ball, put into a bowl, cover with a cloth and leave to rise for 3–4 hours.

Then add the rest of the flour, oil, sugar, remaining 2 eggs and a pinch of salt. Work well in, adding a little warm water, until you have a good soft dough. Now add the finely chopped candied peel and small grapes (which should have been left to soften in warm water for not more than 15 minutes and then dried).

The dough is now kneaded hard for a while and then divided into long sticks to form small but longish loaves. Arrange these on a well-oiled cookie sheet and leave to rise for a few hours. Then cook in a very hot oven for about 15 minutes.

3 oz bread dough	*3 tablespoons sugar*
1 lb flour	*3 tablespoons candied peel*
pinch of salt	*1 cup small grapes* or
2½ tablespoons cooking oil	*sultanas*
3 eggs	

Savoy Cookies

Beat the sugar and egg yolks in a bowl working vigorously until the mixture is thickened and fluffy. Separately, beat the egg whites to a firm snow, then fold in the yolk mixture, the vanilla sugar, flour and cornstarch. Divide the mixture into little bun or muffin tins which have been well buttered and floured: fill them only two-thirds full. Cook in a moderate oven and serve cold.

2¼ cups sugar	*1¼ cups flour*
7 eggs (separated)	*1¼ cups cornstarch*
1 teaspoon vanilla-flavored sugar	

Family Cookies

Mix the flour, butter, sugar, bicarbonate of soda, vanilla powder, powdered sugar, pinch of salt and the milk, to a paste.

Above: cookies can be any variety
of shape to please children.

Jam ravioli.

Working vigorously, knead the dough for a while then roll out to a thickness of about 1 in. Cut out shapes as you please from this to make as many cookies as you can. Decorate by pricking lightly with a fork. Arrange on a floured baking sheet and put into a hot oven to brown.

Easy to make, these cookies go very well with early morning tea or coffee.

2 cups flour	1 sachet vanilla powder
2 tablespoons butter	1 teaspoonful powdered sugar
2 tablespoons caster sugar	pinch of salt
good pinch of bicarbonate of soda	½ cup milk

Bocca di Dama (Lady's Mouth)

Using a pestle and mortar, crush the peeled and blanched almonds. Add the spoonful of caster sugar. Then mix in the flour.

Beat the egg yolks with the 1 cup of sugar and the grated lemon peel. After 15 minutes incorporate the almond and flour mixture, working it in carefully for another 30 minutes. In a separate bowl beat the egg whites to a firm snow, then fold in the mixture. Turn into a buttered and floured pie plate and cook in a hot oven. It is cooked when a knitting needle inserted into it will come away clean.

2 tablespoons sweet almonds with a few bitter ones	3 egg yolks
1 tablespoon caster sugar	1 cup sugar
1¼ cups flour	grated peel of 1 lemon
	6 egg whites

Cold Zabaione

In a bowl mix the egg yolks, sugar, marsala, grated lemon peel, pinch of powdered clove and pinch of vanilla powder.

Cook in a bain-marie over a moderate heat until creamy and fluffy. Take off the heat and leave to cool.

In a separate bowl, whip the cream and then fold it into the cold Zabaione. Pour into individual serving bowls, decorate with a wafer and a cherry or strawberry in the center or a dob of whipped cream.

6 egg yolks	*grated peel of ½ lemon*
½ cup sugar	*pinch of powdered clove*
¾ cup marsala	*pinch of vanilla powder*
¾ cup cream	

Turkish Tart

In a bowl first of all mix the flour and sugar and then add the milk, melted butter and finally brandy, mix well to obtain a smooth mixture. When this is achieved add the grated lemon peel and pine kernels and sultanas (previously softened if necessary in a little warm water). Beat the egg whites to a firm snow and fold them carefully into the mixture. Last of all add the yeast dissolved in a little water. Stir for a few seconds longer to incorporate the yeast then turn into a well buttered oven pan to cook for at least 45 minutes in a moderate oven.

The Turkish tart is ready when a knitting needle inserted in it will come out clean. It is taken out, left to cool and dusted with caster sugar.

2 cups flour	*grated lemon peel*
½ cup sugar	*2 tablespoons sultanas*
½ cup milk	*2 egg whites*
2 tablespoons butter	*1 envelope dried yeast*
½ small glass brandy	*caster sugar*
1 tablespoon pine kernels	

Elevenses

Fried Rice

Boil the milk with an equal quantity of water. When just boiling throw in the rice. When it is quite cooked take the pan off the heat and leave to go cold. Now add the grated orange peel, sugar, flour, yeast and powdered clove. Stir well and leave to rise for at least 1 hour. Then spread the mixture out on a slab. Divide into pieces of any shape you like (square, round, diamond, etc.). Pick up with a spatula and drop singly into very hot oil for a few minutes.

3 cups milk	*1 cup flour*
1 lb rice	*½ packet yeast*
grated orange peel	*pinch of powdered clove*
2 tablespoons sugar	*oil for frying*

Cheese Tart

Beat the eggs in a bowl, add the grated cheese, 4 spoonfuls of flour, 1 of sugar, the saffron and a pinch of salt. Mix it all up thoroughly.
Turn the mixture into a buttered pie plate then cook in a hot oven for about 20 or, at the most, 30 minutes. Turn the pie onto a plate and dust with sugar. It is usually served hot but some people prefer it cold.

3 eggs	*1 tablespoon sugar*
1 lb pechorino cheese	*saffron*
(or cheddar)	*pinch of salt*
4 tablespoons flour	*sugar*

Fruit tartlets.

Ricotta Cheese Tart

Work the Ricotta and sugar well together (this takes quite a long time) then, still stirring, add the egg yolks, then the flour, grated lemon peel and baking powder.

Beat the egg whites to a firm snow, then fold them carefully into the mixture. Turn into a buttered pie pan and put into a pre-heated moderate oven to cook until a knitting needle inserted in the tart will come out clean. Ricotta cheese tart is served cold dusted with sugar.

1 cup fresh Ricotta cheese	*grated peel of 1 lemon*
1 cup sugar	*2 teaspoons baking powder*
2 eggs (separated)	*sugar*
2 cups flour	

Fruit Barquettes

Make shortcrust pastry as described in the basic recipe chapter, to the quantity given below. Roll out to about $\frac{1}{4}$ in. thick. Use to line little buttered barquette pans. Put into the oven to cook and when done leave to go cold.

Take the barquettes out of the pans; glaze the insides with melted chocolate couverture and then fill with Frangipani cream or pastry cream (see Basic Recipes) topping them with the fruit of your choice.

If you wish, the barquettes may be decorated with fruit glaze and chopped, toasted almonds.

1 lb shortcrust pastry	*seasonal fruit*
$\frac{1}{4}$ lb chocolate couverture	*fruit glaze (optional)*
Frangipani or pastry cream	*toasted almonds (optional)*

Maize Bread

Mix half the measured quantity of white flour with the yeast, dissolved in warm water, to a paste. Shape into a round loaf and leave to rise.

Meanwhile mix the remaining white flour and the corn flour with the sugar, butter, fat and a pinch of salt; binding the whole with enough warm water to make it the consistency of bread dough.

Maize bread.

Ricotta cheese tart may be used as the basis
for an elaborate pie.

When it is well risen add the flour and yeast loaf to the other dough, kneading it in hard. Lastly mix in the small grapes or sultanas (previously softened in water if necessary). Then divide the dough into about 15 parts making each one into a small round loaf. Cut a cross on top and leave to rise in a warm place. Having risen they are then placed on a buttered and floured cookie sheet and cooked in a moderate oven. Take care not to let them dry up.

$2\frac{1}{2}$ cups white flour	1 tablespoon cooking fat
$\frac{3}{4}$ packet yeast	salt
1 cup fine corn flour	1 cup small grapes or
2 tablespoons sugar	sultanas
1 tablespoon butter	warm water to mix

Rice Tartlets

Cook the rice in the milk stirring as it thickens so it does not stick together. After about 15 minutes add the sugar, butter, chopped candied peel and a pinch of salt. Leave to cook until the rice is almost soggy; remove from the heat; leave to go cold and then add the rum, egg yolks, and lastly the egg whites beaten to a firm snow. Dust a few muffin pans with breadcrumbs; fill with the rice mixture and cook in a moderate oven. The rice tartlets are served cold.

$\frac{3}{4}$ cup rice	1 tablespoon chopped candied peel
$3\frac{1}{4}$ cups milk	salt
$2\frac{1}{2}$ tablespoons sugar	$2\frac{1}{2}$ tablespoons rum
1 tablespoon butter	3 eggs (separated)

Classic Ricotta cheese tart.

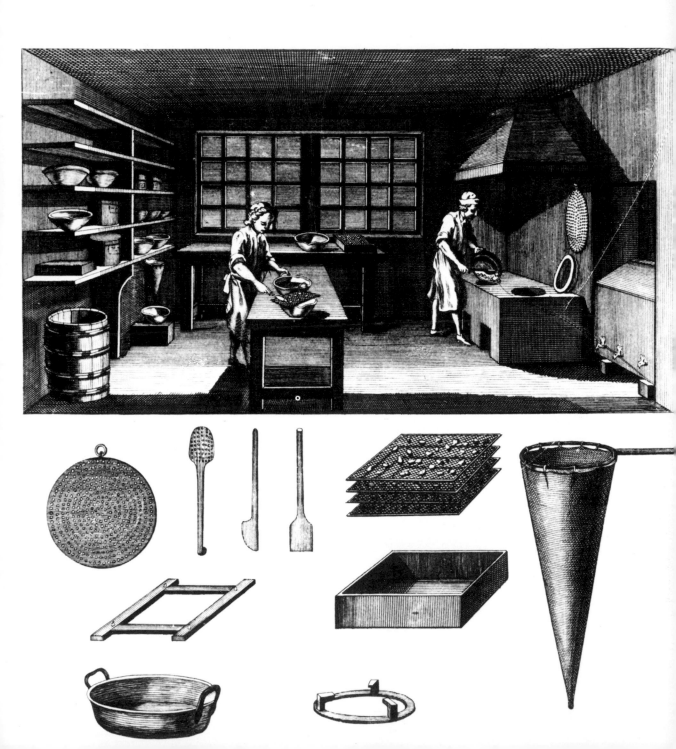

Midday

Sweet Polenta Fritters

Pour the milk into a saucepan with the sugar and a pinch of salt. Heat until just boiling then add the flour and continue to cook, stirring all the time, for about 20 minutes.

Take off the heat, add the butter, and egg yolks and lemon peel, stirring again for a few minutes.

Spread the mixture thinly out on a damp slab so it is about $\frac{1}{2}$ in. thick. Now cut it out into squares, rectangles or any shapes which can be coated with egg and breadcrumbs and dropped into a hot deep pan to fry. It is best to cook a few at a time.

The polenta fritters are drained, dusted with powdered sugar and served immediately.

3 cups milk	*$2\frac{1}{2}$ tablespoons butter*
$\frac{1}{2}$ cup sugar	*3 egg yolks*
salt	*lemon peel*
$1\frac{1}{4}$ cups flour	*beaten egg, breadcrumbs, oil for frying*

Rice Fritters

Bring the milk to the boil, throw in the rice and leave to cook for about 10 minutes. Now add the butter, sugar, pinch of salt and grated lemon peel.

Leave to boil up until the rice is well cooked, then turn it out into a bowl. When the rice is cold, mix in the egg yolks, flour and rum and stir well.

In a frying pan heat a good amount of olive oil. While this is heating, beat the egg whites to a firm snow and fold into the rice mixture. When the oil is really hot drop in the mixture

Following page: Fruit Salad Pie.

49

in teaspoonfuls. The fritters are cooked when both sides are just golden, then they should be drained and arranged on absorbent paper.

2½ cups milk	grated lemon peel
½ cup rice	3 eggs (separated)
1 tablespoon butter	½ cup flour
1 tablespoon sugar	2½ tablespoons rum
salt	oil for frying

Apple Fritters

Slice the apples about ⅕ in. thick, after peeling and coring. Arrange on a plate and sprinkle with half the sugar. Make a paste with the remaining sugar, the milk, a spoonful of flour, the eggs, baking powder and grated lemon peel. Dip the apple slices in this one at a time; then throw into very hot deep fat until golden all over.

They are served very hot after being drained on absorbent paper.

6 or 8 apples (according to size)	2 eggs
2 tablespoons sugar	1 teaspoon baking powder
½ cup milk	grated peel of 1 lemon
flour	oil for frying

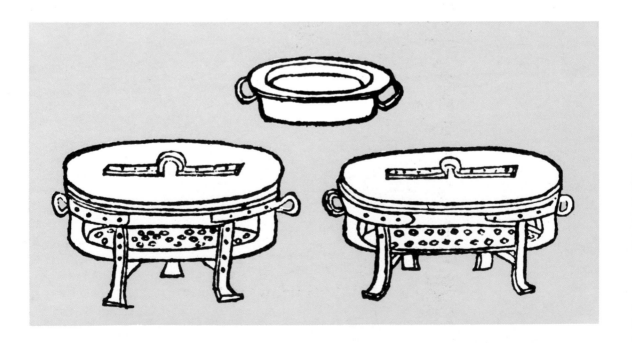

Grape Fritters

Put the washed grapes into a bowl and flavor with a small glass of rum or Ricard. In another small bowl dissolve the yeast in half a glass of warm water with the sugar and a little of the flour and leave to rise. Add the rest of the flour to this risen paste and more water until you have a slightly runny dough.

Now add the chopped nuts, sliced citron, salt, grated lemon peel and finally the grapes. Mix vigorously for a while, then leave to rise covered with a cloth, in a warm place.

When the dough has doubled in volume drop teaspoons of it into deep hot fat and cook until well-browned on both sides. Dip into vanilla sugar and then drain on absorbent paper.

1 cup small yellow or green grapes	*2 tablespoons candied citron*
1 small glass rum or Ricard	*salt*
1¼ packet yeast	*grated peel of 1 lemon*
2½ tablespoons sugar	*oil for frying*
1 lb flour	*vanilla sugar*
2 tablespoons chopped edible pine nuts	

Yeast Tea Bun

Put the flour into the oven for a few seconds to warm. Pour onto a smooth slab and add the yeast which has been diluted in a glass of warm water. Mix to a dough adding as much water as is necessary to make a soft but homogeneous dough.

Put the dough into a bowl and leave to rise in a warm place. When it has doubled in volume add the egg yolks, sugar, melted butter, milk and a pinch of salt. Mix well for a while, then incorporate the grapes which should have been softened in water. Turn the dough into a buttered pie plate, leave to rise for another hour, then cook in a pre-heated moderate oven for about 40 minutes.

1¾ cups flour	*2 tablespoons butter*
¾ packet yeast	*1 tablespoon milk*
2 egg yolks	*pinch of salt*
½ cup sugar	*½ cup small green grapes*

Tondone

Put the flour in a bowl with the pinch of salt and mix, little by little, with enough water to make a runny dough.

Melt a knob of butter in a frying pan, then pour in the batter and cook, turning halfway through, but taking care that it does not brown.

The Italians call the resultant pancakes *Tondone* ("rounds"). The pancakes are then broken into tiny pieces, mixed with 2 eggs and the grated lemon peel, and the whole crushed together. This mixture is then turned into a bowl and the yolks of the remaining four eggs mixed in. Now add the grapes, previously softened in a little water, and beat the egg whites to a firm snow and fold them in.

Teaspoonfuls of the mixture are dropped into a frying pan full of hot oil and cooked until the fritters are golden brown all round. Drain on absorbent paper. Dust with fine sugar and serve very hot.

2¼ cups flour	grated peel of 1 lemon
pinch of salt	1 cup small green grapes
knob of butter	oil for frying
6 eggs	fine sugar

Potato Fritters

Boil and cream the potatoes. Leave to go cold. Add the eggs, sugar, flour, grated lemon peel, baking powder and pinch of salt. Stir vigorously.

Drop the mixture in teaspoonfuls into a pan of very hot fat. Leave the fritters to brown evenly on both sides, then drain on absorbent paper.

Dust with fine sugar and serve immediately.

2 lb potatoes	1 teaspoon baking powder
3 eggs	salt
1 cup sugar	oil for frying
1 cup flour	fine sugar
grated peel of 1 lemon	

Chestnut Fritters

Pour the powdered chestnut and flour into a bowl and mix with the oil, grapes (previously softened in water and dried), vanilla powder and enough water to make a slightly runny dough. Mix for a while, then leave to stand for a few hours. The chestnut fritters are cooked by dropping teaspoonfuls of the mixture into hot oil and must cook until they have formed a crusty outer skin.

They are drained on absorbent paper and served hot or cold.

1 lb powdered chestnut and flour mixed	*1 envelope vanilla powder*
1¼ cups olive oil	*oil for frying*
½ cup small green grapes	

Surprise Ring

Warm the milk, then add the butter stirring until it melts. Set aside. Beat the egg yolks with the sugar and, separately, whip the whites to a firm snow. Carefully fold the whites into the yolk mixture.

Turn the flour into a big bowl. In the center put the egg mixture, the milk and melted butter, the grapes (previously softened in water), candied peel and aniseed. Stir well until you have a good smooth mixture.

Turn into a buttered ring mold, glaze with beaten egg yolk and put into a moderate oven. The ring is cooked when it is a good golden brown color. Take out and leave to cool before serving.

½ cup milk	*1 lb flour*
½ cup butter	*½ cup small green grapes*
3 eggs (separated) and 1 extra yolk	*½ cup mixed candied peel*
¾ cup sugar	*pinch of aniseed*

Polenta Pizza

Beat the Ricotta with a little warm water in a small bowl. Still stirring add the sugar, then little by little the flour, until you have a smooth thick paste. Then add the grapes (previously softened in a little water) and a pinch of cinnamon.

Turn into a pie plate, greased with shortening or oil, sprinkle the top with nuts and dot with margarine. Put into the oven and cook for 1 hour, by then it should be done. Leave to go cold before serving.

3 cups Ricotta cheese	*cinnamon*
1 cup sugar	*oil for greasing*
3½ cups fine-grain wholemeal flour	*2 tablespoons pine nuts*
½ cup small green grapes	*shortening*

Sweet Ricotta Patties

Mix the Ricotta well in a bowl with the sugar, broken-up chocolate, diced candied fruit and a pinch of cinnamon.

Make a dough, separately, by mixing the flour with the eggs and roll it out to about $\frac{1}{8}$ in. thick. Then cut out small circles, using a glass or metal pastry-cutting shape. In the center of each put a teaspoonful of the Ricotta mixture then fold the dough up over it, sealing the turned over flap.

Throw the little patties into very hot oil to cook until golden. They are served dusted with vanilla-flavored powdered sugar and piping hot.

$2\frac{1}{2}$ cups Ricotta cheese	$2\frac{1}{2}$ cups flour
$\frac{3}{4}$ cup powdered sugar	2 eggs
$\frac{1}{4}$ cup chocolate	oil for frying
$\frac{1}{2}$ cup mixed candied fruit	vanilla powder and sugar mixed
cinnamon	

Chestnut Tart

Mix the chestnut flour in a bowl (it is best to sieve it first to avoid lumps) with two table-spoonfuls of oil, the sugar, a pinch of salt and enough water to make a rather fluid paste. Pour the mixture into a well-oiled baking pan. The mixture should be quite shallow. Sprinkle with rosemary, pine nuts, and the grapes (previously softened in water and dried).

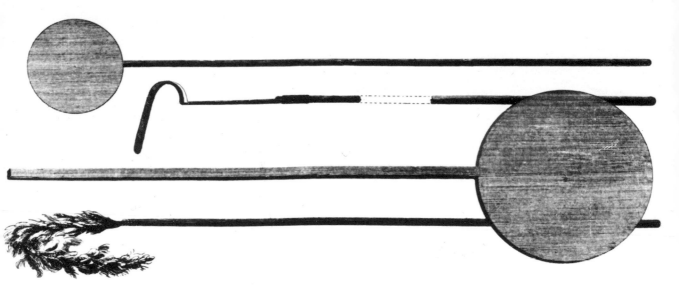

Brush the top with oil and put into the oven, leaving to cook for one hour or until it has formed a nice dark brown crust.

It may be eaten cold but hot it has that inimitable *olde worlde* country flavor.

2 cups chestnut powder and flour mixed	fresh rosemary
olive oil	$\frac{1}{2}$ tablespoon pine nuts
$\frac{1}{2}$ tablespoon sugar	$\frac{1}{2}$ tablespoon small green grapes
salt	

Sweet Ravioli

Put the flour into a bowl, making a well in the centre. Put in the egg yolks, pinch of salt and enough warm water to mix to a smooth paste. Knead well and roll out into a square. Pour enough melted butter over half the dough to cover it and fold over the other half. Roll out again and fold over and repeat this operation another 4 or 5 times to get it quite smooth. Finally roll out to about $\frac{1}{8}$ in. thick.

Make the filling as follows: finely chop the orange peel, pumpkin and candied citron and bind together with the marrow. Stir well to get a good mixture. Arrange teaspoonfuls of the filling at regular intervals on half the dough, cover with the other half. Cut out the ravioli using a pastry cutter.

The ravioli are fried in hot, deep oil and served hot dusted with sugar.

$3\frac{1}{2}$ cups flour	peel of 1 orange
2 egg yolks	2 tablespoons candied citron
pinch of salt	$\frac{1}{2}$ cup candied pumpkin
1 cup butter	$\frac{3}{4}$ cup meat-bone marrow

Simple Bun Ring.

Pizza Booklets

Mix the flour with the eggs, pinch of salt and three tablespoonfuls of brandy to a paste. Roll out to a rectangle about $\frac{1}{8}$ in. thick. Spread with melted butter and fold it over itself so that the butter is on the inside. Cut into little squares from top to bottom. Press down with the fingers hard on the uncut edge of each little square and throw into deep hot oil to fry.

You will see that as they cook the little squares open up like so many little books. When they are golden brown, drain them, place on absorbent paper and serve dusted with sugar.

1½ cups flour	1 tablespoon butter
2 eggs	oil for frying
salt	sugar
4 tablespoons of brandy	

Country-Style Cake

Put the butter, sugar, eggs, grated lemon peel, vanilla, baking powder and salt into a bowl. Mix vigorously for a few minutes.

Sieve the flour into a bowl and make a well in the centre. Turn the mixture into this, mix to a smooth paste with the milk and leave to stand for about 30 minutes.

Make the dough into the shape of a round cake and place on a buttered and floured metal cake pan. Cook in a moderate oven for at least 40 minutes.

This cake is eaten cold.

1¼ cups butter	2½ tablespoons baking powder
1¼ cups sugar	pinch of salt
4 eggs	2 lb flour
grated peel of 1 lemon	1 cup of milk
pinch of vanilla powder	

Two-Flour Tart

Mix the two kinds of flour in a bowl with the sugar, the egg yolk, a pinch of salt, the milk and the rum. Stir well until you have a smooth mixture; then incorporate, working carefully, two egg whites beaten to a firm snow. Dissolve the baking powder in a little milk and add it to the mixture.

Turn the mixture into a buttered and floured cake pan and cook in a hot oven for about 30 minutes.

This tart is served either hot or cold.

1 cup corn flour (i.e., flour made from corn)	pinch of salt
1 cup wheat flour	1½ cups milk
1 tablespoon caster sugar	1 tablespoonful rum
1 egg (separated)	1 teaspoon baking powder
1 extra egg white	

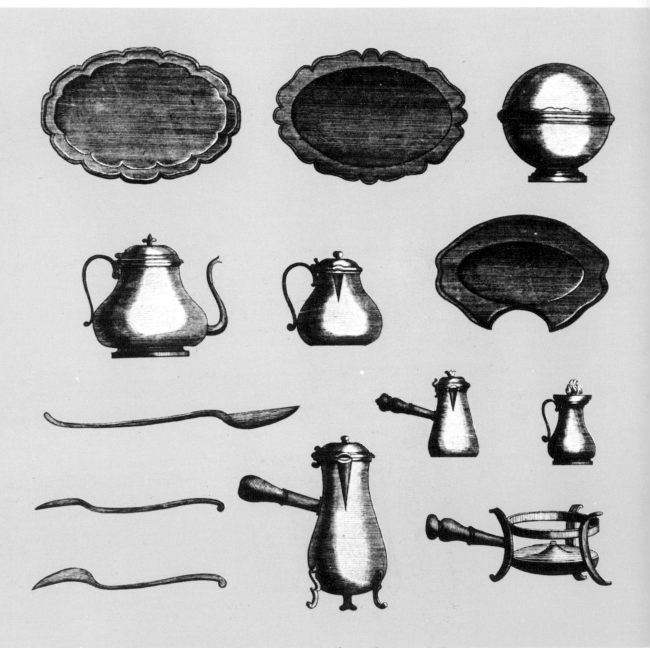

Afternoon Tea

Macaroons

Grind the almonds in a bowl with half the sugar using a mortar. After a few minutes add one egg white, mix up well and add the rest of the sugar, the second egg white and the Kirsch.

Form the dough into small rounds and arrange on wax paper on a buttered cookie sheet. Put into the oven and leave to cook at a moderate heat for at least 30 minutes.

Macaroons are eaten cold, preferably the day after cooking. They may be kept for quite a long time in a sealed tin.

$\frac{1}{2}$ cup almonds	2 egg whites
1 cup sugar	1 small glass of Kirsch

Cats Tongues

Beat the egg whites to a firm snow. Fold in the sugar and flour. Mix for a few seconds, then add the whipped cream and a little vanilla-flavored sugar. Only mix for as long a time as is absolutely necessary.

Fill a forcing bag with the mixture and squeeze out strips of mixture (about 4 in. long) on a buttered and floured cookie sheet, taking care to space them well apart. Cook in a moderate oven for about 10 minutes. They are best eaten cold.

4 egg whites	$2\frac{1}{2}$ tablespoons whipped cream
$\frac{1}{2}$ cup caster sugar	vanilla-flavored sugar
1 cup flour	

Crumiri

Mix the brown and white flour together with the sugar, vanilla powder, 4 egg yolks and the butter. Stir well, form into a ball and leave to stand for 30 minutes. Divide the dough into three pieces and put them one by one into the forcing bag with a star-shaped nozzle. Squeeze out in little stick shapes, each about 4 in. long, onto a well buttered and floured cookie sheet, lightly bending them in the middle. Cook them in a hot oven until they are light gold in color. They are delicious with afternoon tea.

2½ cups brown flour	1 envelope vanilla powder
1¾ cups white flour	4 egg yolks
¾ cup sugar	1¼ cups butter

Savoyards

Beat the egg yolks and the sugar in a bowl, then add the flour, little by little, and the pinch of salt. Beat the egg whites to a firm snow and carefully incorporate them. Make sure that the mixture is smooth, then put into a forcing bag with a non-serrated nozzle. Squeeze out onto a buttered cookie sheet in 4 in. lengths, well spaced out so that they don't stick together while cooking. Dust with powdered sugar and put into a hot oven.

6 eggs (separated)	pinch of salt
¾ cup sugar	powdered sugar
1¼ cups flour	

Crunchy Almond Cookies

Slowly mix the flour, egg, egg yolks, sugar, butter, brandy, and bicarbonate of soda, adding if necessary warm water. Stir a little, then add the peeled and blanched almonds, aniseed, pine nuts, chopped candied peel and grapes. Mix well, then shape into a long roll to be sliced and laid out on a buttered and floured cookie sheet.

Tea cookies for every taste.

Cook in a hot oven for approximately ten minutes so that the slices remain soft. Then cut each slice into small pieces and put these pieces again onto a buttered cookie sheet in the oven to turn golden brown and crunchy.

3½ cups flour	1 teaspoon bicarbonate of soda
1 egg	2 tablespoons almonds
3 egg yolks	pinch of aniseed
¾ cup sugar	1 tablespoon pine nuts
3 tablespoons butter	1 tablespoon candied peel
2½ tablespoons brandy	2 tablespoons small green grapes

Little Almond Cakes

Mix the sugar, powdered almond, flour and pinch of salt in a bowl. Beat the egg whites to a firm snow and fold in the almond mixture.
Soften the butter and add to the mixture with the grated lemon peel.
Butter some muffin pans, fill with the mixture and cook in a moderate oven for 30 minutes. Take them out of the muffin pans while still hot and leave to cool before eating.
They keep well in a sealed tin.

1½ cups sugar	9 egg whites
1 cup powdered almond	¾ cup butter
1½ cups flour	grated peel of a lemon
pinch of salt	

Vanilla Cookies

Crush the almonds, sugar, stick of vanilla and a little flour together using a pestle and mortar. Add a little water to make a thick paste.
Turn this out onto a slab dusted with fine sugar and roll out to ¼ in. thick. This is then covered with a thin layer of icing (see Basic Recipes) and cut into several small wide strips about 4 in. long.
Arrange on a buttered cookie sheet and cook in a moderate oven. Take out as soon as they turn dark in color—probably after about 10 minutes.

1 cup almonds	a little fine flour
¾ cup sugar	icing (see Basic Recipes section)
stick of vanilla	

Turkish Mahallebi

Pour the rice and enough water to cover into a saucepan and boil up until the grains are quite soft. Drain the rice, reserving the cooking liquid. When this is cold add the starch, sugar, cream and finally the rice. Heat through again, stirring all the time. Remove from the heat when the cream begins to resist the spoon. Continue to stir.
Serve in small dessert bowls dusted with powdered sugar and sprinkled, if possible, with a little rose water.

$\frac{1}{4}$ cup rice	$2\frac{1}{2}$ cups fresh cream
$1\frac{1}{4}$ cups rice starch	rose water
1 cup powdered sugar	

Cream Meringue

This method can only be used in an electric oven *(Translator's Note)*.
Whip the egg white with $\frac{3}{4}$ cup of sugar. When well fluffed up gradually add the remaining sugar. Arrange in the shape of two rounds of meringue, about 8 in. in diameter, on a buttered and floured cookie sheet. Pre-heat the oven to 180°, then switch it off, put in the meringue and leave the door slightly open. The meringue must dry out in the oven for about 2 hours.
Meanwhile whip the cream; when it begins to thicken add the sugar little by little. Put half the cream on to the meringue round, cover with the other and cover this with the remaining cream.
Decorate with little cookies, candied fruit, etc.

6 egg whites beaten to a firm snow	$3\frac{1}{2}$ cups cream
$1\frac{1}{4}$ cups sugar	2 tablespoons sugar

Coffee Viennoise

This is iced coffee or more properly, ice cream with coffee.
To make it put 2 or 3 scoops of vanilla ice cream in a bowl, and serve with the same

Cream meringue.

amount of expresso coffee in a small cup and a bowl of chantilly cream. Each person pours the coffee over the ice cream, adding cream according to taste.

vanilla ice cream	*chantilly cream*
expresso coffee	(see Basic Recipes section)

Meringues with Ice Cream

Make meringues according to the basic recipe (page 30). Cut the top off each one. Fill with a couple of blobs of vanilla ice cream, top with chantilly cream and the meringue lid and serve. You may add a cherry or other fruit if wished.

meringues	*chantilly cream*
vanilla ice cream	(see Basic Recipes section)

Eclairs

First of all prepare $\frac{3}{4}$ lb of choux pastry (see Basic Recipes chapter). Pour the choux pastry into a forcing bag with a medium nozzle. Butter and flour a cookie sheet and squeeze out

onto it as many éclair-shaped lengths of paste as possible. They should be about 3 in. long and fairly widely spaced. Brush with beaten egg and put into a moderate oven for about 15 minutes. At the end of this time turn off the heat and leave them in the oven for another 2–3 minutes. Take them out, cut a slit in them lengthways; ice with melted chocolate and fill with the cream of your choice: chantilly or pastry cream etc. . . .
The icing may also be varied if you wish.

$\frac{3}{4}$ *lb choux paste*	*chocolate couverture*
1 egg	*cream*

Plum Cake

Soften the butter and mix it in a bowl with the sugar, then mix in the eggs one at a time. Continue to stir until the mixture is smooth and well integrated. Now add the roughly chopped dried fruit, sultanas, grated lemon peel, baking powder (dissolved in a little water) and lastly the rum. Mix vigorously, pouring in the flour at one go and taking care that it is all thoroughly mixed in. Line a cake pan with buttered wax paper and fill to three quarters full with the cake mixture. Cook in a moderate oven.

1 cup butter	*grated peel of 1 lemon*
1 cup sugar	*1 teaspoon baking powder*
4 eggs	*2$\frac{1}{2}$ tablespoons rum*
$\frac{1}{2}$ cup dried fruit	*2$\frac{1}{4}$ cups flour*
1 cup sultanas	

English Scones

This is a delicious Italian version of English scones! *(Translator's Note)*.
Put the flour into a bowl, making a well in the center. Put in the baking powder, softened butter, sugar dissolved in the milk, pinch of cinnamon and grated lemon peel. Mix to a dough. Stir hard for a few minutes and then divide the mixture into individual rounds about 4 in. in diameter. After a few minutes standing, slightly flatten the rounds with a rolling pin but retaining their circular shape. Cut into 4 (by cutting across again to make wedge shaped pieces).

Place scones on a buttered and floured cookie sheet, brush with beaten egg and put into a hot oven for 10 minutes.

$1\frac{1}{4}$ lb flour	$1\frac{1}{2}$ cups milk
1 tablespoon baking powder	cinnamon
3 tablespoons butter	grated peel of $\frac{1}{2}$ lemon
3 tablespoons sugar	1 egg

Orange Cookies

Mix the flour with the sugar, softened butter and egg. Work well until you have a smooth homogeneous mixture. Then add the diced candied orange and grated lemon peel. Form into long narrow shapes then arrange them on a buttered and floured cookie sheet; glaze with beaten white of egg; dust with sugar and put into a pre-heated moderate oven for not more than 20 minutes.

$2\frac{1}{4}$ cups flour	2 tablespoons candied orange
$\frac{1}{2}$ cup sugar	grated peel of 1 lemon
2 tablespoons butter	1 egg white
1 egg	sugar

Belgian Waffles

Put the flour into a bowl; make a well in the center and put in the eggs, sugar, pinch of salt and yeast dissolved in a little milk. Mix to a paste, adding milk little by little as necessary, until you have a soft well-mixed mixture, and lastly add the melted butter; stir for a few minutes longer and then cover with a cloth and leave to rise in a warm place for at least 2 hours until it has doubled in volume.

The waffles may be cooked in a traditional waffle iron or, failing this, on a buttered griddle iron. In this case cook each side in turn for a few minutes until quite firm, turning like a pancake, using about 1 tablespoon of the mixture at a time.

$2\frac{1}{4}$ cups flour	$\frac{1}{2}$ packet yeast
2 eggs	milk
$1\frac{1}{2}$ tablespoons sugar	2 tablespoons butter
pinch of salt	

Madeleine

Dice the fruit roughly and put into a bowl. Pour over the Kirsch and leave to macerate for a while. Then add the ice cream and Chantilly cream (see Basic Recipe), mixing up well. Pour into a rectangular gelatin mold and put into a freezer and leave to freeze for several hours.

Turn out onto a serving dish and decorate lavishly with whipped cream.

$\frac{1}{2}$ cup candied fruit	$2\frac{1}{2}$ cups vanilla ice cream
$\frac{1}{2}$ small glass Kirsch	$1\frac{1}{2}$ cups chantilly cream

Puff Pastry Fans

Make $\frac{3}{4}$ lb puff pastry (see Basic Recipe). Roll out to a rectangle. Then fold the dough over itself so that the shortest sides of the rectangle meet flush with each other in the

A variation on puff pastry fans.

70

centre. Fold over again in the same way so that you now have 4 long narrow layers of dough.

Out of this cut as many little slices as possible about ½ in. in width, taking care not to open them up. Arrange on a buttered oven sheet, propping them on end and leaving a good space between each. Put into a hot oven to cook for a few minutes until the dough dilates and the fans open up. A few minutes before taking them out, dust with extra fine sugar which will melt and caramelize.

Take care not to leave them in the oven too long.

¾ lb puff pastry	extra fine sugar

Ladies' Kisses

Using a pestle and mortar, crush the almonds with a pinch of sugar. Mix to a paste with flour, butter and remaining sugar. Divide the mixture into little nut sized pellets and put onto a buttered cookie sheet in a pre-heated moderate oven for at least 15 minutes. Melt the chocolate in a bain-marie and dip the base of one little cookie in it, using this dab of melted chocolate to stick it to a second cookie. Continue until all the little cookies are paired up in this way.

1 cup toasted almonds   *1 cup sugar*
2 cups flour   *2 tablespoons bitter chocolate*
1 cup butter

Cocktail and Apéritif Snacks

Snowballs

Boil the milk and drop in teaspoonfuls of the egg whites beaten to a firm snow with a third of the measured-out sugar. When they are cooked take out with a draining spoon. Take the milk off the heat, add the remaining sugar and a tablespoon of flour; stir and leave to go cold. Beat the egg yolks with a fork and add them to this mixture.
Shell the pistachio nuts and soften them in a little extra boiling milk; drain them and add them to the milk and egg yolk mixture. Heat through again but do not boil.
Arrange the firm egg white "snowballs" on a plate. Cover them with the mixture flavored with a little cinnamon.

2¼ pints milk	1 tablespoon flour
4 eggs (separated)	1 tablespoon pistachio nuts
2½ tablespoons sugar	cinnamon

Little Rings

Pour the flour into a bowl; add the sugar, finely chopped lemon peel and a pinch of salt. Then mix in the eggs, bicarbonate of soda and the cream of tartar dissolved in a little white wine. Beat hard, adding the melted butter, little by little, until you have a smooth well-mixed paste.
Divide into 30–40 little rings which are arranged on a buttered cookie sheet and cooked in a moderate oven for about 15 minutes.

1¼ lb flour	pinch of bicarbonate of soda
½ cup sugar	pinch of cream of tartar
peel of 1 lemon	a little white wine
pinch of salt	½ cup butter
2 eggs	

Pineapple Pie.

Venetian Baicoli

Make a fairly firm dough with about $\frac{3}{4}$ cup of the flour, the fresh yeast and a little warm milk. Shape into a ball. Make 2 cross-cuts on the top. Put into a bowl, cover with a cloth and leave to rise in a warm place for at least 30 minutes. At the end of this time mix together the remaining flour, the butter and sugar, 2 pinches of salt and the beaten egg white. Incorporate the risen dough. Mix well together adding more and more milk until you have a dough which is the softness of bread dough.

Work this in by hand, then divide it into four parts, each one of which is shaped into a long, narrow cylinder. Arrange these, well spaced out, on a buttered cookie sheet. Cover and leave to rise again for about 1–2 hours. They are then cooked in the oven for 10 minutes. They are left to go cold before being removed from the cookie sheet and finally left to stand, covered with a cloth, for about 2 days. Then they are sliced diagonally in very thin pieces. These are then put back into the oven and crisped. They are eaten cold and will keep for a long time.

$\frac{1}{2}$ packet yeast	2 tablespoons sugar
$3\frac{1}{2}$ cups flour	salt
milk	1 egg white
2 tablespoons butter	

Filoncini

Shred the almonds. Put the flour into a bowl and add the eggs, sugar, a pinch of baking powder and a pinch of salt. Mix well and stir in the almonds vigorously for a few minutes; then divide the mixture into pieces the shape of Hot Dog rolls.

Arrange these on a buttered and floured cookie sheet and put in the oven. When barely browned cut them into diagonal strips and return to the oven until cooked through.

1 cup toasted almonds	1 lb sugar
1 lb flour	pinch of baking powder
4 eggs	pinch of salt

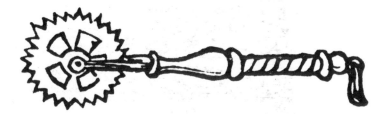

Marzipan Fruits

Crush the almonds in a bowl with a few teaspoons of sugar, using a mortar until they are quite powdered. Strain through a fine sieve into a bowl adding three-quarters of the measured glucose and mixing up well.

Separately, melt the remaining glucose with the sugar, removing it from the heat as soon as it begins to color. Then pour it over the almond mixture in the bowl. Mix thoroughly; when quite cold, moisten with a little water and then press through a fine sieve several times until quite soft and smooth. Shape as you wish: into little fruits; figures; people etc. . . . Leave them to dry out for a few days after which they may be painted or decorated with artificial colorants, and then (after being left again for a day or so) varnished with gum arabic dissolved in a little water.

You won't get professional results at the first try. But you will have fun making up unusual subjects!

1 cup skinned almonds	*artificial coloring*
2 lb sugar	*gum arabic*
1½ cups glucose	

Candied Orange Peel

Cut each orange in half and separate the peel from the pulp so that the former is unbroken. Cut the peel in half again and leave for at least 2 days to soak in cold water. Drain and drop into boiling water and when barely tender, drain and dry. Cut into interesting shapes. Heat an equivalent amount of sugar in a pan and when caramelized add the peel, mixing carefully. After a few minutes turn out onto a lightly oiled slab; separate and leave to go cold.

oranges	*sugar*

Stuffed Dates

Peel and blanch the almonds, then crush them using a pestle and mortar. Add the Kirsch and mix to a paste.
Make a sugar syrup (see Basic Recipe) and mix into the almond paste. Put this mixture into the refrigerator and take it out when quite cold. Cut into small pieces and fill the split pitted dates with them.

½ cup almonds	*2 tablespoons sugar syrup*
½ small glass Kirsch	*24 dates*

Caramelized Chestnuts

Shell the chestnuts and throw into lightly salted boiled water. Take them out when they feel tender if tested with a fork. Drain and peel them. Dry them and leave for at least one whole day.
At the end of this time, melt the sugar gently in a pan and dip the chestnuts one by one into the caramel thus made (see Basic Recipes). Arrange on a slightly damp plate and leave for a few hours before serving.

chestnuts	*sugar*
salt	

Delicate little pastries for an elegant snack.

After the Theatre

Drunken Eggs

Beat the egg yolks with the sugar until they are thick, then add the wine gradually, measuring two half eggshells per yolk. This makes a delicious and most nourishing beverage.

4 egg yolks	*½ cup sugar*
red wine	

Mascarpone with Liqueur

Beat the egg yolks with the sugar until they are white. Add gradually the *mascarpone* and flavor with a small glass of liqueur. Whip the egg whites until very stiff and fold them into the beaten yolks a spoonful at a time, stirring delicately.
Chill for a long time then serve in a bowl.

4 egg yolks	*3 egg whites*
1¼ cups sugar	*1 small glass liqueur*
1¼ cups mascarpone *(a very rich cream cheese)*	

Poppy Seed Cake

Beat the eggs with the sugar and when they are white and frothy add the flour and starch sieved together.
Pour the mixture onto a buttered sheet of wax paper spread over a baking tray. It should

Poppy Seed Cake.

Opposite page: Caramel Creams.

be about ⅕ in. thick. Cook in a very hot oven for 20 minutes.

Turn out and allow to cool.

Meanwhile blend the apricot jelly with the poppy seeds which should have been lightly roasted in the oven. Spread this over the cake, roll it over, wrap it in wax paper and chill. To serve, cut into slices and eat with whipped cream.

6 eggs	*1 cup apricot jelly*
¾ cup sugar	*1 lb poppy seeds*
¾ cup flour	*whipped cream*
2 packets starch	

Drunken Chestnuts

Roast the chestnuts in the special perforated pan; when ready peel carefully and put on a plate.

Cover the plate with a cloth soaked in red wine. Keep in a warm place for about 30 minutes, then eat the chestnuts, washing them down with some more wine.

chestnuts	red wine

Ricotta Ravioli

Make some shortcrust pastry according to the Basic Recipe, shape it into a ball and allow to stand for 1 hour. Meanwhile beat the *Ricotta* with the sugar, 3 egg yolks, a pinch of cinnamon, a little grated lemon peel and 2 tablespoons of rum, until the cream is blended and thick.

Roll out the dough to a thickness of about $\frac{1}{4}$ in. and cut it into fairly large discs about 4 in. in diameter. Fill these with the cream, fold over carefully with the fingers or with a fork, brush with beaten egg and cook in a hot oven, on a buttered baking tray.

The ravioli will be ready when they have turned golden and passed the knitting needle test.

For the shortcrust pastry	For the filling
$1\frac{3}{4}$ *cups flour*	*1 cup Ricotta*
$\frac{1}{2}$ *cup butter*	*1 tablespoon confectioners sugar*
$\frac{1}{2}$ *cup sugar*	*3 egg yolks*
4 egg yolks	*cinnamon*
lemon peel	*grated lemon peel*
	$2\frac{1}{2}$ *tablespoons rum*
	1 egg yolk for glaze

Pineapple Dessert

Cube the pineapple, sprinkle it with Kirsch and Maraschino and leave it to macerate for a while. Mix it with the vanilla ice-cream and fill some dessert bowls completely with this mixture. Put in the centre of each bowl a small meringue topped with a dollop of ice-cream; cover the whole thing with a strawberry purée flavored with Kirsch and surrounded with Chantilly cream.

tin of pineapple (1 slice per person)	*purée of strawberry (4 tablespoons per person)*
Kirsch and Maraschino	*crème chantilly (4 tablespoons per person)*
vanilla ice-cream (1 scoop per person)	
meringues (1 per person)	

Bocconcini

Heap up the flour and work it into a paste with 4 egg yolks, the sugar and the lard. Knead well, then roll out to a thickness of at least $\frac{1}{4}$ in. Butter and flour some small round baking tins about 3 to 4 in. in diameter, or sprinkle them with breadcrumbs. Line them with small rounds cut out of the dough, very slightly larger in diameter than the molds themselves. Separately in a bowl mix the jam, the chocolate, the chopped citron, the grated lemon peel, the vanilla sugar, a few spoonfuls of your favorite liqueur and the powdered coffee. When all these ingredients are well blended spread onto the dough in the molds. Cover with other rounds of dough and use a fork to press the edges together.

Brush with beaten egg and cook in a very hot oven for at least 30 minutes. Serve cold.

1¾ cups flour	½ cup unsweetened or baking chocolate
4 egg yolks	¼ cup glacé citron
1 cup sugar	grated lemon peel
1 cup lard	1 sachet vanilla sugar
½ cup peach	liqueur
or apricot jam	1 teaspoon powdered coffee

Almond Wafers

Chop the roasted almonds and mix them with the sugar and the egg whites, stiffly beaten. Flavor with a little cinnamon. Put the vanilla wafers onto a buttered baking tray and arrange a tablespoon of almond mixture in the center of each wafer.

Dust with confectioner's sugar and cook for 15 minutes in a moderate oven.

½ cup roasted almonds	cinnamon
1¼ lb caster sugar	vanilla wafers
3 egg whites	confectioner's sugar

Coupe Marie Thérèse

Slice the bananas finely and sprinkle with the Kirsch and Maraschino, leaving them to soak for at least 1 hour.

Arrange the bananas at the bottom of dessert bowls and cover with strawberry ice-cream.

4 ripe bananas	1 small glass Maraschino
1 small glass Kirsch	¾ lb strawberry ice-cream

Baked bananas.

Flambéed Bananas

Peel the bananas and cut them in two lengthwise. Melt the butter in a baking dish, arrange the bananas in it side by side and cook them over moderate heat for 3 or 4 minutes on each side.

Remove from the heat, dust with sugar, sprinkle with the warmed rum and flambé. Serve at once.

6 bananas	3 tablespoons confectioner's sugar
2 tablespoons butter	a glass of rum

THE FOUR SEASONS

Spring

Sweet Milk Fritters

Beat 3 egg yolks and the lemon peel with the sugar. Mix the flour and milk in a saucepan. Add 3 whole eggs and the egg yolk mixture. Boil for about 1 hour, stirring all the time, then pour into a deep, moistened dish and leave to cool.

When the mixture is cold, cut into smallish diamond shapes, dip into beaten egg whites and breadcrumbs and fry in oil. Coat with icing sugar and eat hot.

6 eggs	*breadcrumbs for coating*
grated lemon peel	*oil for frying*
¾ cup sugar	*icing sugar*
1 cup flour	
1½ pints milk	

Doughnuts

Soften the baker's yeast in lukewarm water, then work it in a bowl with a little flour and a tablespoon of the sugar. Leave to rise. Heap the flour on the rolling board, add 2 egg yolks, the melted butter, the sugar, the rum and the leavened dough. Work well, gradually adding enough milk to obtain a barely smooth mixture. Leave it to rise until it has doubled its volume, then roll out the dough about ¾ in. thick. Cut out rounds and pair them up with a little jam in between. Press firmly the edges of each pair together. Leave them to rise a little more, covered with a floured cloth. After about 30 minutes deep fry the doughnuts on moderate heat. Serve hot, sprinkled with vanilla-flavored sugar.

1 packet baker's yeast	*rum to taste*
2½ cups flour	*milk*
3 tablespoons sugar	*jam*
2 egg yolks	*vanilla-flavored sugar*
3 tablespoons butter	

Custard Fritters

Beat 5 egg yolks with the sugar in a saucepan, then, stirring all the time, add the flour, the grated lemon peel and gradually the milk. Heat, still stirring; when it starts to boil, remove from heat and pour the custard onto a marble slab covered with a film of oil. Allow to cool, then cut into rhombs or diamond shapes, dip into beaten egg whites and breadcrumbs and fry in a boiling mixture of oil and butter. Serve hot.

5 eggs (separated)	2¼ pints milk
¾ cup sugar	seed oil for frying
2 cups flour	butter for frying
grated lemon peel	breadcrumbs for coating

Cherry Tart

Beat the eggs with the sugar, add the sifted flour, the vanilla and the melted butter.
Pour the mixture into a round buttered and floured cake pan and cook in a hot oven for at least 30 minutes.
Allow to cool, then unmold and slice into two equal discs. Trim about ¾ in. from all round the edge of the top disc.
Now prepare the filling, beating the egg yolks with the sugar, adding the flour, the milk (boiled and still warm) and the grated peel. Cook over moderate heat, stirring continuously until the mixture is quite thick. Moisten the two discs with liqueur, spread with filling, dot the larger disc with cherries and cover with the smaller disc.
Use more cherries to decorate the edge of the smaller disc and heap up a few in the centre of the cake.

For the pastry	For the filling
5 eggs	5 egg yolks
1 cup sugar	¾ cup sugar
2¼ cups flour	½ cup flour
pinch of vanilla	2½ cups milk
knob of butter	grated peel of 1 lemon
liqueur for moistening	1¼ cups cherries (pitted)

Sablé

Cream the butter with the sugar until the mixture is creamy and frothy. Add 3 egg yolks. Still beating, add the starch and flour mixed with a pinch of yeast; then fold in the stiffly beaten egg whites. Season with a pinch of salt and grated lemon peel.

Butter a baking pan, sprinkle it with breadcrumbs, pour in the mixture and cook in a hot oven for 30 minutes. Do not open the oven during the cooking.

The *sablé* is delicious cold and, like most cakes, it tastes better still if eaten the next day.

$1\frac{1}{4}$ cups butter	$1\frac{1}{4}$ cups flour
$1\frac{1}{4}$ cups sugar	pinch of yeast
3 eggs (separated)	pinch of salt
$\frac{3}{4}$ cup starch	grated lemon peel

Rice Cake

Heat the milk in a saucepan with the sugar and grated lemon peel. When it comes to the boil add the rice and salt. Once the rice has absorbed all the milk remove from heat and allow to cool. Blanch the almonds, peel and chop them, then add them, with the egg yolks, to the rice mixture, stirring vigorously. Fold in the stiffly beaten egg whites. Pour the mixture into a buttered cake pan sprinkled with breadcrumbs and cook in a slow oven for about 40 minutes.

$2\frac{1}{4}$ pints milk	pinch of salt
$\frac{1}{2}$ cup sugar	$\frac{1}{2}$ cup almonds
grated lemon peel	a few bitter almonds
1 cup rice	4 eggs (separated)

Raspberry Dessert

Butter a tall, smooth-sided mold about 8 in. in diameter. Mix the raspberry jam with the Kirsch.

Make a syrup with the sugar, half a glass of water and 8 tablespoons of Kirsch. Steep the ladyfingers one by one in the syrup, line the bottom of the mold with them and spread a layer of jam over them. Add another layer of ladyfingers, followed by another layer of jam and so on until the mold is filled up. The last layer should be of ladyfingers.

Cherry Tart.

The look of a sweet is as important as
its taste.

Cover with a weighted plate and chill for at least 1 day. Prepare the glaze by mixing the sifted confectioner's sugar with the egg white, adding a spoonful at a time until it is all used up; then add 4 tablespoons of Kirsch and the raspberry syrup.

Unmold the dessert and pour the glaze over it in an irregular pattern. Decorate to taste with glacé fruit and serve with fresh cream.

1 lb ladyfingers	For the glaze
1½ lb raspberry jam	1 egg white
4 tablespoons Kirsch	1½ cups confectioner's sugar
fresh cream	½ cup Kirsch
For the syrup	2½ tablespoons raspberry syrup
½ cup sugar	
½ glass water	
1 cup Kirsch	

Sweet Pizza (Ricotta Pie)

To make the pastry, mix the flour with the sugar, the lard and the egg yolks. Form into a ball, place on oiled paper and stand in a cool place for at least an hour. In a saucepan mix ½ cup of sugar, ½ cup of flour and 1 egg and dilute with half a glass of milk. Cook over moderate heat, stirring constantly. Remove from heat, beat in 1 egg yolk and a little grated lemon peel. Add this to the sieved *Ricotta* and the blanched, peeled and chopped almonds.

Divide the dough into two. Roll out the larger piece and line a floured and buttered pie plate with it. Fill with the egg and *ricotta* mixture. Roll out the second piece of dough, cover the tart, pressing the edges together. Brush a little beaten egg yolk on the top and cook in a medium oven for 30–40 minutes. Serve cold, sprinkled with confectioner's sugar.

For the filling	For the pastry
½ cup sugar	2½ cups flour
½ cup flour	¾ cup sugar
2 eggs	¾ cup lard
½ glass milk	3 egg yolks
grated lemon peel	beaten egg for glaze
1 cup Ricotta cheese	
½ cup almonds	

Strawberry Bavarois

Boil the milk, remove from heat and infuse with the vanilla stick for 15 minutes.
Soften the isinglass in lukewarm water and squeeze dry. Beat the eggs with ½ cup sugar,

adding the milk gradually and finally the isinglass. Cook over moderate heat, stirring until the mixture coats the spoon: do not let it boil. Remove from heat and pour through a very fine sieve into a bowl. Leave to cool. Whip the cream with $\frac{1}{4}$ cup sugar. Add it to the mixture, then the remaining $\frac{1}{4}$ cup of sugar, the puréed strawberries and the whole *fraises des bois*. Mix a little more and pour into a moistened *bavarois* mold (if possible; otherwise use a round cake pan). Chill for a few hours.

To serve, dip the mold for a moment in boiling water, reverse carefully onto a dish and unmold delicately.

1¼ cups milk	*2½ cups whipped cream*
a stick of vanilla	*½ lb strawberries*
1 teaspoon isinglass	*2 tablespoons* fraises des bois
1 cup sugar	*(wild strawberries)*
2 egg yolks	

Flamri

Pour the wine and water into a saucepan and bring to the boil. Sprinkle in the semolina and leave to cook over moderate heat for about 20 minutes. When this time has elapsed add the sugar, the whole egg and the stiffly beaten egg whites. Stir until the mixture is smooth and remove from heat. Butter a mold, pour in the mixture and allow to cool. To serve, unmold onto a dish, cover with a purée of strawberries and decorate with cherries or other glacé fruit.

1¼ cups white wine	*3 egg whites*
1¼ cups water	*strawberries*
¾ cup semolina	*cherries*
¾ cup sugar	*glacé fruit*
1 egg	

Yugoslav Semolina Dessert

Chop the almonds finely and put in a saucepan with the semolina. Heat, stirring all the time, until the mixture turns golden. In another saucepan put the water, the sugar and the butter and bring to the boil. Pour the boiling liquid slowly onto the almond and semolina mixture, stirring all the time. When all the liquid has been absorbed the result should be a rather thick cream. Cover the saucepan, first with a cloth, then with the saucepan lid, and allow to cool. Moisten some small molds with a little water and pour in the mixture. Leave to stand a little longer. (It may also be chilled.)

Unmold onto individual plates, dust with vanilla-flavored sugar and serve.

$\frac{1}{2}$ cup chopped almonds	$1\frac{1}{4}$ cups sugar
$\frac{3}{4}$ cup semolina	$\frac{3}{4}$ cup butter
2 pints water	1 tablespoon vanilla-flavored sugar

Strawberries Cardinal

Clean the strawberries carefully. Clean the raspberries, sieve them into a bowl and mix with the sugar and the orange and lemon juice.

Arrange the strawberries in the serving dish or in individual fruit bowls. Sprinkle them with the Kirsch and cover them with the raspberry purée. Decorate with a few pistachio nuts.

1 lb large strawberries	juice of $\frac{1}{2}$ lemon
$\frac{1}{2}$ lb raspberries	small glass Kirsch
1 cup confectioner's sugar	1 tablespoon pistachio nuts
juice of $\frac{1}{2}$ orange	

Coupe Romanoff

Moisten the strawberries with the orange juice and the curaçao and macerate for at least 30 minutes.

In the meantime prepare the Chantilly: whip the chilled cream; when it is thick fold in delicately the powdered sugar and the vanilla-flavored sugar. Chill again or keep in a cool place if not used immediately. Arrange the macerated strawberries in fruit bowls and cover with Chantilly.

$\frac{3}{4}$ lb strawberries	$2\frac{1}{2}$ cups fresh cream
juice of 2 oranges	$\frac{1}{2}$ cup powdered sugar
small glass of curaçao	1 tablespoon vanilla-flavored sugar

Summer

Peaches with Cocoa

Cut the peaches in half, remove the pits, scoop out a little flesh and put it on one side. Chop up the almonds and the macaroons, mix them with the peach flesh and add the sugar and the cocoa. Fill each peach half with this mixture, dot with small pieces of butter, moisten with muscat wine and dust with sugar. Place the peaches on a buttered cookie sheet and put into a hot oven for about 40 minutes. Serve hot.

6 peaches	*1 tablespoon cocoa*
1 tablespoon almonds	*butter*
½ cup crushed macaroons	*1 glass muscat wine*
2 tablespoons sugar	*sugar for dusting*

Peach paste dessert

Blanch the peaches, peel them and remove the pits. Pass them through a sieve and put the resulting purée in a saucepan. Add the same weight in sugar and bring to the boil, stirring all the time, until the mixture browns. Line the bottom and sides of a baking pan or mold with wafers; pour in the mixture, dust with sugar and put to dry for some time in a moderate oven, keeping its door open.
Remove, allow to cool, then chill for at least three days. Eventually unmold the sweet, cut it into rectangles, dust again with sugar and serve.

peaches	*wafers*
sugar in equal weight	

A selection of party treats.

Water Melon Fruit Salad

Cut out two large wedges from the top of the water melon rind so as to leave a "handle" shape. Scoop out all the flesh with a spoon but without exposing the white rind underneath. Remove the seeds and cube the flesh. Cube the other fruit also, mix these with the water melon flesh and add the sugar and the cognac. Fill the water melon with the fruit salad and put onto a serving dish.

Garnish with small ice cubes and decorate with leaves.

1 round, ripe water melon	1 small glass cognac
mixed fruit in season	ice cubes
5 tablespoons sugar	leaves for decoration

Strawberry Sponge Cake

Clean the *fraises des bois* carefully. Reserve a few and moisten the others with 2 small glasses of Kirsch. Sprinkle them with sugar and add a little water.

Garnish the sponge cake with the macerated strawberries, cover with whipped cream, decorate with the remaining strawberries and dust with the powdered sugar. This delicious cake should be served chilled.

$\frac{1}{2}$ lb fraises des bois	1 sponge cake weighing about $\frac{1}{2}$ lb
(wild strawberries)	1 cup whipped cream
2 small glasses Kirsch	powdered sugar
$\frac{1}{2}$ cup sugar	

Oats Pudding

Roast the oatmeal flakes in the oven for a few minutes, then mix them with the milk and cook on top of the stove for about 15 minutes, stirring all the time. Allow to cool and sift through a fine cloth into a bowl. Beat the 4 egg yolks with the sugar, add them to the oats and continue to cook, stirring continuously until the mixture thickens. Dip a metal bowl into cold water, pour in the mixture and chill for quite a long time. Unmold before serving.

2 cups oatmeal flakes	4 egg yolks
$2\frac{1}{2}$ cups milk	$\frac{1}{2}$ cup sugar

Alba Cake

Beat the eggs with the sugar and add the flour, the milk, the lemon peel and the dried yeast, stirring all the time.

Pour the mixture into a buttered metal bowl sprinkled with breadcrumbs. Add the peeled and finely sliced apples on top and sprinkle with sugar. Dot with tiny pieces of butter and cook in a moderate oven for about 45 minutes.

2 eggs	*lemon peel*
¾ cup sugar	*1 teaspoon dried yeast*
1½ cups flour	*2 lb apples*
2½ tablespoons milk	*½ cup butter*

Zuppa Inglese (Italian Trifle)

Make a *crème pâtissière* (according to the Basic Recipe section), preparing the quantity given below. When it is ready, reserve a few spoonfuls, and add the chopped glacé fruit to the rest.

Cut the sponge cake into slices about ½ in. thick. Take the cream you set aside and spread it onto a baking dish, add half the sponge slices, sprinkle them with the alkermes and cover with the *crème pâtissière* and glacé fruit mixture. Arrange another layer of sponge slices over this and moisten them with rum.

Beat the egg whites with powdered sugar until stiff and spread on the top of the sweet. Decorate with candied orange and lemon peel and sprinkle with powdered sugar. Cook in a moderate oven for a few minutes until the meringue becomes golden. Serve well chilled.

1¼ lb crème patissière	*1 small glass rum*
½ cup glacé fruit	*3 egg whites*
½ lb sponge cake	*1½ cups powdered sugar*
1 small glass alkermes	*candied lemon or orange peel*
(liqueur colored red with cochineal)	

Zuccotto

Prepare a 1 lb sponge cake (see the Basic Recipe for Genoese Pastry). Allow to cool, remove the crust and slice it horizontally into two identically thick discs. With one of these line a semi-spherical mold (a large pot will do equally well). Moisten the sponge cake with the rum, Kirsch and cognac all mixed together.

Whip the cream, add the peeled and chopped almonds, the chopped hazelnuts, $\frac{3}{4}$ cup of the powdered sugar and the chocolate flakes, folding them in with care. When all the ingredients are well blended divide the mixture into two halves. Melt the chocolate in a double saucepan and add it to one of these.

Spread a layer of the cream mixture evenly over the sponge cake in the mold and fill the central cavity with the chocolate mixture. Top with second layer of cake.

Chill well. Just before serving unmould the *zuccotto* onto the serving dish and sprinkle with powdered sugar and powdered cocoa, making the white and brown pattern characteristic of this sweet.

1 lb sponge cake	$\frac{1}{2}$ cup hazelnuts
1 small glass rum	1 cup powdered sugar
1 small glass Kirsch	1 cup chocolate flakes
1 small glass cognac	$\frac{1}{4}$ lb cooking chocolate
2 pints fresh cream	powdered cocoa
$\frac{1}{2}$ cup almonds	

Ricotta Cassata

Blanch the almonds in boiling water, reserving about 10. Peel, chop and pound them in a mortar. Roast the remaining 10 and chop them.

Make a caramel syrup with the sugars and a few spoonfuls of water. Line a few small, ladle-shaped molds with sponge cake and moisten with alkermes.

Mix the *Ricotta* with the almonds, the chopped glacé fruit and the caramel syrup, add a pinch of cinnamon, the grated lemon peel and finally the chocolate broken up into small pieces. Blend all together just a little and fill the molds with this mixture. Chill long enough for the mixture to become quite firm.

Unmold the *cassata* just before serving and cover with a thin layer of almond paste which may be bought ready made.

1 cup almonds	$\frac{3}{4}$ lb Ricotta *cheese*
2$\frac{1}{2}$ cups caster sugar	2 tablespoons glacé fruit
1 cup sugar	pinch of cinnamon
$\frac{3}{4}$ lb sponge cake	grated lemon peel
alkermes (liqueur colored red	2 tablespoons cooking chocolate
with cochineal)	almond paste

Water Melon Fruit Salad.

Below: Apple tart.

Figs à la Carlton

Peel the figs, cut them into two, arrange them in a bowl and chill. In the meantime clean the raspberries carefully, blend them into a purée and add powdered sugar to taste. Fold in the Chantilly (see page 20) and cover the figs with the mixture.

12 fresh figs	powdered sugar
1 cup raspberries	2 cups crème Chantilly

Almond Milk

This is a delicious beverage which is particularly refreshing on very hot days. It is extremely popular in southern countries and its origins go back to ancient times.
Blanch and peel the almonds and pound them thoroughly in a mortar. Pour the paste into a glass jar and cover with water up to several inches above the mixture. Put in a cool place and stand for at least 1 day. Then filter it through a cloth. The almond milk is then ready and should be drunk very cold.

almonds	water

Sweet Wheat

Soak the wheat for at least 12 hours, then drain and boil it until soft. Drain it once again, put it in a bowl and add a few spoonfuls of sugar, some grated chocolate, grated walnuts, even a few pomegranate seeds, and enough boiled wine to soften the mixture.
Mix well, chill and serve in a bowl.

wheat	walnuts
sugar	pomegranates
chocolate	boiled wine

Melon Ice

Choose a fine melon, making sure it is sweet and ripe. Cut it and scoop out all the flesh. Sift this through a fine mesh into a bowl. Add the sugar, a pinch of cinnamon, the orange-flower water, the chocolate and the minced candied citron. Mix well together, put into a metal bowl and freeze. Unmold a little before serving and sprinkle with powdered cinnamon.

$4\frac{1}{2}$ lb melon flesh	1 small glass orange-flower water
$\frac{3}{4}$ cup sugar	1 cup flaked chocolate
cinnamon	$\frac{1}{2}$ cup candied citron

Apricots with Cream

Wash the apricots and cut in half, removing the stones. Boil the water with the sugar flavored with a pinch of vanilla and put in the apricots, a few at a time. Remove them after 5 minutes and drain well.

In the meantime moisten the macaroons with the liqueur and using the cream and the sugar, prepare a Chantilly cream (according to the Basic Recipe section).

Arrange the drained apricots on a serving dish, cover each one with a little Chantilly cream and top with a macaroon. Pile the remaining cream in the center of the dish and arrange the rest of the macaroons in a circle around it.

10 large ripe apricots	20 macaroons
1 glass water	1 small glass Maraschino
1 cup sugar	$2\frac{1}{2}$ cups single cream
pinch of vanilla	1 cup sugar for Chantilly cream

Apricots with whipped cream.

Cherry Dessert

Beat the egg yolks with the sugar until frothy. Add the breadcrumbs, the sherry and the lemon peel. Beat a little longer, then fold in the stiffly beaten egg whites. Last, add the blanched, peeled and chopped almonds. Pour the mixture into a buttered cake pan sprinkled with breadcrumbs and arrange the cherries on top (these should be washed and dusted with flour but not dried, so that they do not sink too deeply into the mixture). Cook in a hot oven.

4 eggs	*lemon peel (finely grated)*
1 cup sugar	*2 tablespoons sweet almonds*
1 cup breadcrumbs	*2 cups cherries*
2 tablespoons sherry	

Stuffed Peaches

Divide the peaches in half, remove the pits and scoop out the holes a little with a small knife or some other appropriate implement. Pound the blanched and peeled almonds in a mortar with 2 tablespoons of the sugar. Add them to the crumbled ladyfingers and the finely chopped candied citron. Mix well and fill the peach halves with this. Pour the wine and remaining sugar into a baking pan and arrange the peaches in it. Cook in a moderate oven.

These stuffed peaches may be eaten hot or cold, served in the syrup in which they were cooked.

6 peaches	4 ladyfingers
2 tablespoons sweet almonds	1 tablespoon candied citron
3 tablespoons sugar	small glass white wine

Sweet Tomato Preserve

Blanch the tomatoes in boiling water, peel them carefully, cut them in half and remove pips. Melt the sugar in a saucepan with a few spoonfuls of water over moderate heat. As soon as it is melted, add the tomatoes, the lemon juice and a little of its grated peel. Continue to cook over moderate heat, stirring often: when the mixture becomes fairly thick, add the vanilla-flavored sugar and remove from heat.

The preserve is now ready. It should be stored in jars and used like jam.

$2\frac{1}{4}$ lb tomatoes	juice of 1 lemon, and a little peel
$1\frac{1}{4}$ cups sugar	1 envelope vanilla-flavored sugar

Iced Melon

The success of this recipe depends on the quality of the melon: it should be not too large, fragrant and above all just ripe.

Cut a lid from the top of the melon, remove the seeds and filaments and scoop out all the flesh with a spoon. Put the flesh in a bowl, sprinkle with some of the sugar and the Kirsch and Maraschino combined. Sprinkle the inside of the melon with sugar and fill it with alternate layers of melon flesh and orange or lemon ice until all the ingredients are used up. Replace the lid and chill well before serving.

1 medium-sized melon	$2\frac{1}{2}$ tablespoons Maraschino
1 tablespoon sugar	$\frac{3}{4}$ cup orange or lemon ice
$2\frac{1}{2}$ tablespoons Kirsch	

Creole Cream

Wash the sultanas carefully, drain and macerate in a cup with the rum.

Mix the *Ricotta* with the sugar and egg yolks in a bowl; when they are blended add the rum and the sultanas. Beat the egg whites until they are very stiff and fold them carefully into the mixture. Pour into small fruit bowls, decorate with glacé cherries and chill before serving.

¼ *cup sultanas*	½ *cup sugar*
2½ *tablespoons rum*	*4 eggs (separated)*
1 cup Ricotta *cheese*	*glacé cherries*

Peaches Alexandra

Choose ripe juicy, white peaches, one per person. Blanch them in boiling water, drain immediately and put them in a bowl of iced water, with some ice cubes. Remove the peaches and peel the thin skin by rubbing them with a napkin. Put them on a plate, dust with sugar and chill.

When the peaches are cold, prepare a sugar syrup flavored with a little vanilla powder (see page 27) and throw in the peaches. Leave them to soak until both fruit and syrup have cooled.

Scoop the vanilla ice-cream into the bottom of individual fruit bowls, add a peach per bowl, cover with a purée of strawberries sweetened and flavored with Maraschino and, as a final touch, sprinkle red and white rose petals previously crystallized in sugar over the whole thing.

white peaches	*strawberry purée with Maraschino*
vanilla sugar syrup	*rose petals*
vanilla ice-cream	

Cream Caramel

Boil the milk together with the vanilla stick. Remove from heat as soon as it rises and allow to cool. Meanwhile beat the eggs in a bowl with the egg yolks and ½ cup of sugar. When they have increased their volume add the milk gradually, stirring vigorously to remove any lumps.

Melt the remaining sugar over heat; when it turns red-gold pour it into a metal bowl so that the sides and bottom are completely coated. Fill the bowl with the egg and milk mixture. Cook the pudding in a *bain-marie* in the oven for at least 45 minutes. The cream caramel is ready when it feels thick and elastic. Remove the bowl, allow to cool, then chill. Unmold just before serving, taking great care that the caramel drips from the bowl onto the dessert.

$2\frac{1}{2}$ cups milk	4 egg yolks
$\frac{1}{2}$ stick vanilla	$\frac{3}{4}$ cup sugar
2 eggs	

Oriental Melon

Cut out a lid from the top of the melon. Remove the seeds and filaments and scoop out the flesh with a round-headed scoop so as to obtain small balls of melon flesh. Cut the pineapple into cubes and the bananas into rounds, add to the melon balls in a bowl and sprinkle with Kirsch and sugar, leaving the whole thing to macerate. Chill. When it is well chilled fill the melon with the fruit salad, replace the lid, put onto a serving dish and serve.

1 ripe melon	1 small glass Kirsch
$\frac{1}{2}$ lb pineapple	$\frac{3}{4}$ cup sugar
4 bananas	

Plum and Apricot Tart

Cream the butter with the sugar, the egg, the grated lemon peel and a pinch of salt.
Heap the flour onto a pastry board and add the mixture, working well with the hands so as to obtain a smooth dough in a short time. Cover the dough with a dish towel and allow to stand for at least 1 hour.
After 1 hour roll out the dough to a thickness of $\frac{1}{4}$ in. Line a buttered and floured pie plate with this, pricking the surface with a fork so as to avoid air bubbles. Cook in a hot oven for 20 minutes.
When the pastry is cold, spread a layer of jam over it, add the ladyfingers, then another

layer of jam. Finally top with the plums and apricots arranged in concentric circles. Turn out the tart and place on a serving dish.

1 cup butter	*2½ cups flour*
½ cup sugar	*ladyfingers*
1 egg	*raspberry jam*
lemon peel	*plums*
pinch of salt	*apricots*

Diplomat

Pour the rum, diluted with a few spoonfuls of cold water, into a pan. Place a sheet of wax paper at the bottom of a smooth-sided metal bowl (about 6 in. in diameter), to facilitate the unmolding of the dessert. Cut some of the ladyfingers into triangles, moisten them on one side only with the rum and form them into a star pattern in the bottom of

Peach dessert.

Left: Prune and Apricot tart.

Below: Cream Caramel.

the bowl. Line the sides of the bowl with upright ladyfingers, also moistened with rum on one side only. Make sure they do not rise above the top of the plate.

Fill the inside with a layer of apricot jam; cover with a layer of rum-moistened ladyfingers, and so on; the last layer should be of ladyfingers. Place the bowl onto a plate, weight it with a $\frac{1}{2}$–$\frac{3}{4}$ lb weight over the last layer of ladyfingers and chill for at least a day.

Just before serving unmold onto a dish or crystal bowl and cover with *crème anglaise* (see Basic Recipe section) chilled for a few hours.

3 small glasses rum	apricot jam (sifted)
1 lb ladyfinger biscuits	2½ cups crème anglaise

Fruit Cake

Add the sugar to the butter and then add the eggs and egg yolks, one at a time. Mix well, sprinkle in the flour and starch sifted together, the yeast, the soaked and well drained sultanas and finally the cubed glacé orange.

When the mixture is smooth pour it into a cake pan large enough so that the mixture comes only three-quarters of the way up the sides. Cook in a moderate oven for at least 1 hour. Like all such cakes this should be eaten cold. It may also be dusted with sugar and decorated to taste.

1¾ cups sugar	¾ cup starch
¾ cup butter	1 envelope yeast
2 whole eggs	2 tablespoons sultanas
2 egg yolks	2 tablespoons glacé orange
2 cups flour	

Coconut Cake

Grate the coconut carefully, add the butter, the sugar and a pinch of vanilla. Beat well, then add the eggs, one by one, still beating until the mixture is soft and light

Add the sifted flour a little at a time so as to avoid lumps forming.

Pour the mixture into a high-sided buttered and floured cake pan and cook in a moderate oven for about 25 minutes.

The cake should be unmolded when cold and may be decorated with a little grated coconut.

¾ lb coconut flesh	pinch of vanilla
1 cup butter	8 eggs
1¼ cups sugar	1½ cups flour

Peach Dessert

Add a pinch of vanilla to the milk in a saucepan, then the sugar, a pinch of salt, a knob of butter, and heat. When it starts to boil add the rice and let it cook for about 20 minutes.
Drain, pour into a serving dish and cover with the quartered peaches.
Cover the whole thing with a little apricot jelly and decorate with cherries or other glacé fruit and pistachio nuts.
This peach dessert is good eaten at once and excellent if eaten well chilled.

2 pints milk	1 cup rice
pinch of vanilla	1 tin yellow peaches
2 tablespoons sugar	4 tablespoons apricot jelly
pinch of salt	glacée cherries
knob of butter	pistachio nuts

Date Cake

Mix together the egg yolks, the flour, the sugar, the finely chopped almonds and equally finely chopped dates in a bowl. Fold in the stiffly beaten egg whites delicately.
Pour the mixture in a cake pan smeared with a film of groundnut oil and place into a previously heated oven. Cook over moderate heat for about 25 minutes. This date dessert is delicious eaten cold.

6 eggs (separated)	1 cup almonds
1½ cups flour	1 cup dates
1 cup sugar	groundnut oil for greasing

Fruit cake.

Coconut cake.

Diplomat is a subtle dessert suitable for elegant occasions.

Cold Zabaione.

Date cake.

Flan des îles or Pineapple Pie

Beat the *Ricotta* and add the whole beaten eggs, the sugar, the flour, the orange juice and the pineapple juice from the can.

Mix well, adding the pineapple cubes. Pour the mixture into a buttered pie plate and cook in a *bain-marie* for 45 minutes.

Unmold and, if wished, cover the pie with the pineapple cubes. Chill well before serving.

2 cups Ricotta *cheese*	*1 teaspoon flour*
4 eggs	*juice of 2 oranges*
½ cup sugar	*1 small can pineapple cubes*

Paradise Cake

Beat the butter in a bowl until it is soft and frothy. Add the sugar and vanilla sugar and, beating all the time, ¼ cup of starch and the grated lemon peel. When the mixture is well blended add the whole eggs, still beating away, and the previously beaten egg yolks. Sprinkle in the flour, the remaining starch and the yeast, all sifted together.

Butter and flour a round cake tin, pour in the mixture and cook in a moderate oven for at least 30 minutes. Cut the cake horizontally into two and spread the jam or cream in between.

Serve cold, dusted with powdered sugar.

1 cup butter	*4 egg yolks*
2 cups sugar	*1 cup flour*
½ tablespoon vanilla sugar	*¼ packet yeast*
1 cup starch	*jam or cream filling*
grated lemon peel	*powdered sugar*
4 whole eggs	

Pineapple Condé

Cut the pineapple slices into two, put in a bowl and sprinkle with sugar and Kirsch. Leave to macerate for a few hours.

Prepare some Condé rice (see page 30) in proportionate quantity to the pineapple. Cover it with the macerated slices of pineapple, decorate with glacé cherries or other glacé fruit to taste and pour some Kirsch-flavored syrup over the whole.

1 can pineapple slices	*Condé rice*
sugar	*glacé cherries*
Kirsch	*Kirsch-flavored syrup*

Pineapple Surprise

Cut out a lid from the top of the pineapple. Scoop out most of the flesh with a spoon, leaving just a little on the sides. Pour a small glass of Kirsch inside the fruit, sprinkle in some sugar and keep in a cool place. Cut the pineapple pulp into cubes and put them in a bowl with the fruit salad and the lemon peel. Chill this.

Fill the pineapple with the fruit mixture just before serving. Pour the orange juice over the fruit, replace the lid and arrange in a serving fruit bowl over a layer of finely chopped ice.

1 fresh pineapple	*1 cup fruit salad*
1 small glass Kirsch	*grated lemon peel*
2½ tablespoons sugar	*juice of 1 orange*

Jamaican Cream

Drain the pineapple slices and reserve the juice. Mix the juice in a bowl with the white wine and the sugar. Heat half of this in a saucepan. With the other half dilute the egg yolks mixed with the starch and add the heated liquid, stirring all the time. Pour the whole thing back into the saucepan and let it thicken over low heat, stirring continuously. Finally flavor with Kirsch.

Arrange the pineapple slices in a large fruit bowl, cover with the creamy mixture and decorate with glacé cherries. Chill for at least 1 hour.

1 lb can of pineapple slices	*¾ paket starch*
½ cup dry white wine	*½ cup Kirsch*
1 cup sugar	*½ cup glacé cherries*
4 egg yolks	

Ricotta Whip

Whip the *Ricotta* vigorously. Fold in the cream, the sugar, the egg yolks, the soaked and drained sultanas and the finely chopped glacé fruit. Add the Kirsch. Mix the ingredients delicately and taste, adding more sugar and liqueur if necessary.

Whip the egg whites until they are stiff and fold them carefully into the mixture. Pour into individual bowls, decorate with chopped glacé fruit and put a whole glacé cherry in the center of each bowl. Chill well before serving.

2 cups Ricotta *cheese*	2 tablespoons *sultanas*
1 cup fresh cream	½ cup glacé fruit
½ cup sugar	1 tablespoon Kirsch
3 eggs (separated)	glacé fruit to decorate

Baked Peaches

Cut the peaches in half and remove the pits. Scoop out a little pulp from each with a spoon and mix it with the powdered macaroons, the sugar, the egg yolks and the liqueur. Mix well and fill the peach halves with the mixture, topping each with a peeled almond. Arrange the peach halves in a baking pan, pour in the white wine and cook in a moderate oven for at least 30 minutes.

Remove from the oven, arrange on a serving dish and decorate with whole macaroons or, if wished, glacé fruit.

6 yellow peaches	1 small glass almond liqueur
¼ cup macaroons	12 peeled almonds
½ cup sugar	2 glasses white wine
2 egg yolks	glacé fruit or macaroons to decorate

Sweet Omelette with Cherries

Pick out fine cherries for this dish. Remove the pits and cook the cherries in a sugar syrup (see Basic Recipe section). When they are cooked, drain them and add a little grape jelly.

Beat 4 of the eggs vigorously with a tablespoon of sugar and fry in butter. Put the omelette on a serving dish and dot with the cherries. Make a second omelette with the remaining 2 eggs and cover the cherries with this. Warm up some cognac, pour onto the edge of the omelette, set light to it and serve at once.

2 cups cherries	1 tablespoon sugar
sugar syrup	butter for frying
a little grape jelly	cognac
6 eggs	

Pineapple Condé.

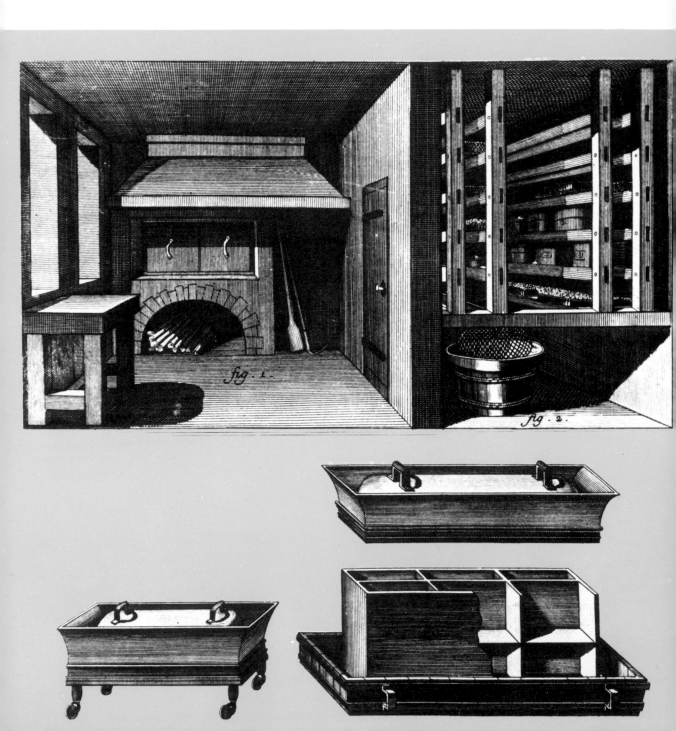

fig. 1.

fig. 2.

Autumn

Brutti Ma Buoni (Almond Cookies)

The name of these cookies literally translated means "ugly but good" *(Translator's Note)*.
Chop the toasted almonds finely, then mix in the stiffly beaten egg whites, the sugar, the
vanilla sugar and a pinch of cinnamon. Cook in a frying-pan over moderate heat, stirring
all the time, for 45 minutes.
Butter a cookie tray and dish out spoonfuls of the mixture on to it. Cook in a moderate
oven for at least 40 minutes. Eat cold.
The cookies may be stored for a long time in a hermetically sealed jar or metal tin.

1 lb toasted almonds	*vanilla sugar*
6 egg whites	*pinch of cinnamon*
1½ cups sugar	

Hazelnut Cake

Put the hazelnuts in a hot oven for a few minutes so that it is easy to peel them. Peel them
and chop them very finely.
Cream together in a bowl the eggs, the butter in small pieces, the flour mixed with the
yeast, the sugar, the chopped nuts, a tablespoon of oil, the milk and the grated peel of a
lemon. Mix thoroughly, pour into a buttered and floured cake pan and cook in a hot oven
for 30 minutes. Serve the cake when it is completely cold.

1 cup shelled hazelnuts	*1 cup sugar*
3 eggs	*1 tablespoon olive oil*
½ cup butter	*¾ cup milk*
2 cups flour	*grated peel of 1 lemon*
1 envelope yeast	

Rough Cake

Mix the flour and the corn-meal with the eggs. Add the peeled and chopped almonds, the sugar, the vanilla and the grated lemon peel. After working the mixture for a few minutes add the shortening and butter in small pieces. Continue to work a little and, with the fingers, tear out small pieces from the dough, dropping them into a buttered and floured cake pan so as to obtain a rough-textured cake. Cook in a hot oven for at least 1 hour. Eat cold, dusted with powdered sugar.

2 cups flour	vanilla flavoring
$1\frac{1}{4}$ cups fine-grained corn-meal	grated lemon peel
2 egg yolks	$\frac{1}{2}$ cup shortening
1 cup almonds	$\frac{1}{2}$ cup butter
1 cup sugar	

Chestnut Cake

This cake may be made with either fresh chestnuts or dried and soaked chestnuts. In either case the chestnuts should be boiled in water, drained, peeled (if they were fresh ones), and put through a food mill or a sieve.

Beat the egg yolks thoroughly in a bowl. Add the sugar, the butter in small pieces, the peeled and chopped almonds, the chestnut purée and the grated lemon peel. Mix vigorously together, then fold in the stiffly beaten egg whites. Pour the mixture into a buttered and floured cake pan and cook in a hot oven for more than 30 minutes.

2 cups fresh chestnuts	$\frac{1}{2}$ cup butter
or 1 cup dried chestnuts	$\frac{1}{2}$ cup almonds
4 eggs (separated)	grated lemon peel
1 cup sugar	

Grape Syrup

This delicious syrup can be stored indefinitely and may be made from any desired amount of ordinary black grapes. It should be remembered, however, that the syrup will weigh about one-third of the original weight of the fruit. Boil the fruit in a metal pot (in the past a copper pot was always used) and leave on the heat, stirring frequently, until its volume is reduced by two-thirds. It may be stored indefinitely in sealed jars—not so indefinitely perhaps if there are children in the house who will undoubtedly be keen to sample this delicious "wine"!

bunch of black grapes

Chocolate nougat.

Panpepato (Nut and Fruit Rolls)

First prepare the dried fruit: blanch the almonds and walnut kernels in boiling water and peel them; roast the hazelnuts for a few minutes and peel them too; soak the raisins for at least 30 minutes. Chop them all roughly, then chop the candied fruit and the chocolate more finely. Add a pinch of salt, pepper and nutmeg. Dilute the honey in a bowl, with a little hot water, add the nuts, dried fruit and chocolate, mix well and gradually add enough flour to make a mixture of the consistency of bread dough. Remove the mixture from the bowl, knead well and divide into small pieces. Shape these into rolls.

Brush the rolls with honey, arrange them on a buttered and floured cookie sheet and cook in a hot oven until they are dark and golden.

2 tablespoons almonds	*pinch of salt*
2 tablespoons walnut kernels	*pinch of pepper*
2 tablespoons hazelnuts	*pinch of nutmeg*
2 tablespoons raisins	*$\frac{1}{3}$ cup honey*
2 tablespoons mixed candied fruit	*flour to mix*
2 tablespoons baking chocolate	

Dried Fig Nougat

Bring the honey to the boil in a saucepan, stirring continuously. As soon as it begins to boil put the saucepan into a container filled with boiling water so that the honey continues to cook in a *bain-marie*. When the honey turns white add gradually the stiffly beaten egg whites which should be slightly warmed up beforehand. The mixture will be of the right consistency when a drop solidifies in contact with water.

Peel and chop the shelled walnuts and the figs. Add them to the honey in the saucepan, with the sugar, a pinch of cinnamon and the grated lemon peel. Continue to stir until the mixture is well blended and thick. Remove the saucepan from the heat and pour the mixture onto a marble slab smeared with a film of seed oil, making sure that the overall thickness is $\frac{5}{8}$ in. When the mixture has cooled a little cut into small rectangles, wrap them in wax paper or, better still, in silver foil and store in hermetically sealed containers.

$1\frac{1}{2}$ lb honey	*1 cup sugar*
2 egg whites	*pinch of cinnamon*
$\frac{1}{2}$ cup shelled walnuts	*grated lemon peel*
2 cups dried figs	*seed oil*

Rice and Chestnut Pudding

Soak the chestnuts for at least 1 day, then drain and clean well. Put them in a saucepan with the milk and cook over moderate heat. After about 30 minutes add the sugar, the rice and the raisins which should have been soaked in lukewarm water and dried.

Stir continuously until the mixture is cooked, adding more milk if necessary to prevent it from becoming too dry. When it is nearly cooked add the butter, stir a little more, then remove from the heat. Pour the mixture into a buttered metal bowl sprinkled with breadcrumbs.

Chill for a long time and unmould just before serving.

$\frac{1}{2}$ cup dried chestnuts	$\frac{3}{4}$ cup rice
2 pints milk	2 tablespoons raisins
2 tablespoons sugar	2 tablespoons butter

Apple Charlotte

Slice up some bread and toast the slices lightly in the oven. Pour melted butter over them and use them to line a well-buttered charlotte mold. Peel, core and slice the apples and cook them in a pan with a knob of butter, 4 spoonfuls of sugar, a little water and the lemon juice. When the apples are soft purée them and add 4 spoonfuls of apricot jam. Pour into the lined mould, making sure it is completely filled as the mixture will reduce greatly during cooking. Cover with a layer of soft crumbs soaked in melted butter and cook in a moderate oven for at least 30 minutes.

When the charlotte is cooked reverse the mold onto a serving dish and wait a few minutes before unmolding.

The apple charlotte should be served hot, accompanied with apricot jam sauce.

bread slices and breadcrumbs	4 tablespoons sugar
$\frac{3}{4}$ cup butter	lemon juice
12 rennet apples	4 tablespoons apricot jam

Apples Bonne Femme

Core the apples carefully without peeling them and make a fine horizontal incision all around.

Arrange them on a buttered cake pan, fill them with a mixture of butter and sugar, pour a little water into the tin and cook in a moderate oven. Serve hot.

6 rennet apples	3 tablespoons sugar
$\frac{1}{2}$ cup butter	

Apple Pie

Peel and core the apples. Cut them into slices $\frac{1}{8}$ in. thick. Prepare some shortcrust pastry (see Basic Recipe section) in the quantity given below and roll it out rather thinly. Line a pie plate with half the rolled-out dough. Arrange the apple slices continuously in a spiral design and dust with sugar and a pinch of cinnamon. Cover with the rest of the rolled-out dough and press the edges together; decorate the edge of the pie with small pieces of extra dough. Prick the surface of the pie with a fork so that it does not burst during cooking, make an incision in the center and cook in a pre-heated moderate oven for at least 40 minutes.

Remove, allow to cool, turn out and serve dusted with sugar.

4 rennet apples	2 tablespoons sugar
$\frac{3}{4}$ lb shortcrust pastry	pinch of cinnamon

Pears Belle Hélène

Peel the pears and soak them in a vanilla-flavored sugar syrup (page 27). Drain and allow to cool. In a fruit bowl, arrange a layer of ice-cream, then the pears and sprinkle with candied violets.

Pears Belle Hélène may be served with a hot chocolate sauce.

6 ripe pears	$\frac{3}{4}$ lb vanilla ice-cream
vanilla-flavored sugar syrup	candied violets

Apple Strudel.

Below: Apple Charlotte decorated
with whipped cream.

Apple Strudel

In a large bowl work the flour with the egg, the oil, a few drops of vinegar and some luke-warm water. When the dough is smooth knead it further on a rolling board until it is perfectly soft, then let it stand for 45 minutes, covered with a warmed salad bowl.
Sprinkle some flour on a fairly large dishcloth. Roll out the dough, then flatten it repeatedly with the back of the hand until it is paper-thin. Brush with melted butter and sprinkle with breadcrumbs browned in butter. Peel the apples and slice them thinly. Mix in the raisins, previously soaked in the rum, the chopped almonds, the sugar and the cinnamon to taste. Spread the filling on two-thirds of the dough, roll up tightly and brush again with melted butter. Cook on a buttered cookie sheet in a moderate oven for 45 minutes.

$2\frac{1}{4}$ *cups flour*	**For the filling**
1 egg	*3 lb apples*
1 tablespoon oil	*3 tablespoons raisins soaked in rum*
a few drops of vinegar	*3 tablespoons chopped almonds*
$\frac{3}{4}$ *cup lukewarm water*	$\frac{3}{4}$ *cup sugar*
2 tablespoons butter	$\frac{1}{2}$ *teaspoon cinnamon*
2 cups breadcrumbs	

Apple Dumplings

Make some very light sweet shortcrust pastry (according to the Basic Recipe)—you will need 2 oz per apple—and roll it out to a thickness of $\frac{1}{8}$ in.
Core the apples, peel them carefully, fill the central cavity with jam to taste (or with butter mixed with sugar and flavored with a pinch of cinnamon), and wrap each individually in a square of dough folded in such a way that it covers the apple completely. Brush the dough with the egg yolk. Place the wrapped apples on a buttered and floured cookie sheet and cook in the oven for at least 45 minutes—the length of time will depend on the size of the apples, as well as their quality.
The dumplings may be served hot or cold.

2 oz shortcrust pastry per apple	*jam*
apples	*1 egg yolk*

Jellied Apples

Peel the apples, core them and soak them in cold water with the juice of $\frac{1}{2}$ a lemon. Dilute the sugar with $2\frac{1}{2}$ cups of water and a spoonful of Kirsch and melt over heat. When it is ready pour it over the apples in a saucepan. Cook on top of the stove, making sure the apples remain whole. When the apples are cooked arrange them on a serving dish. Fill the core-holes with the grape jelly. Reduce the cooking liquid over heat and flavor with another spoonful of Kirsch, and sprinkle over the apples.

2 lb rennet apples (or similar apples)	2½ tablespoons Kirsch
juice of ½ lemon	grape jelly
¾ cup sugar	

Quince Purée

Melt the sugar by boiling it with $\frac{1}{2}$ a glass of water. Peel and core the quinces and slice them very finely. Put them in a saucepan with some water and cook, stirring continuously and crushing the quinces with a wooden spoon so that they soften. When they are practically puréed add the sugar syrup and continue to stir until the ingredients are well blended together.

1 lb sugar	1¾ lb quinces

Cream Cheese Omelette.

Below: Almond Pie Supreme.

Birthday Cake.

Below: Fritters should always be acceptable whatever their size.

Cinnamon Pancakes

Make some pancake batter according to the Basic Recipe section and in the quantities given below. When it is ready allow to stand for 1 hour. Mix the raspberry jam in a bowl with some cinnamon to taste—it is advisable to taste the mixture so as to avoid over-flavoring with cinnamon. When the two are well blended add a pinch of pepper and flavor with some of the rum. This constitutes the filling for the pancakes.

Make the pancakes, frying them in a knob of butter rather than oil. As each pancake gets done fill it with a spoonful of the jam mixture, fold it over and put it in a dish next to the others, dusting each with powdered sugar. Warm the rest of the rum and just before serving pour it over the pancakes and flambé.

For the pancake batter	For the filling and topping
$2\frac{1}{4}$ cups flour	$1\frac{3}{4}$ cups raspberry jam
2 eggs	cinnamon
$2\frac{1}{2}$ cups milk	pinch of pepper
salt	$\frac{1}{2}$ cup rum
2 tablespoons butter	$\frac{1}{2}$ cup powdered sugar

Almond Pie Supreme

Pound the almonds with a little sugar in a mortar.

Heat the flour in a large bowl and add the egg yolks, a pinch of salt, the cream, the remaining sugar, the softened butter and the yeast diluted in a little lukewarm water. Knead the dough energetically and roll out to a thickness of about $\frac{1}{4}$ in.

Line with the dough a buttered pie plate sprinkled with sugar. Spread the almond paste over it and cover with the remaining dough, cut into strips and arrange in a criss-cross pattern.

Brush the surface with a beaten egg yolk and cook in a moderate oven for at least 35 minutes. Decorate with whole almonds.

1 cup peeled almonds and some whole almonds for decoration	pinch of salt
$\frac{1}{2}$ cup sugar	$\frac{1}{2}$ cup cream
$2\frac{1}{4}$ cups flour	$\frac{3}{4}$ cup butter
2 egg yolks	$\frac{1}{4}$ packet baker's yeast

Mixed Fruit Tart

Work the butter, the sugar, the egg and the grated lemon peel together in a bowl with a pinch of salt. Heap the flour on a rolling board, make a well in the center and pour in the mixture and blend together without working too long on it. Cover the dough with a cloth and allow to stand for at least 1 hour.

Roll out the dough to a thickness of $\frac{1}{4}$ in. and line with it a buttered and floured flan tin. Prick the surface with a fork to avoid air bubbles and cook in a hot oven for 15 minutes. When the pastry is cold spread a layer of peach jam over it, arrange the slices of sponge cake in a regular pattern over this and add a little more jam. Decorate with the mixed fruit in a regular pattern and put onto a serving dish.

1 cup butter	3 cups flour
$\frac{1}{2}$ cup sugar	peach jam
1 egg	several slices of sponge cake
grated peel of 1 lemon	fresh fruit in season
salt	

Cream Cheese Omelette

With the spatula work together the cheese, the egg yolk and the sugar. After a few minutes add the crumbled *marrons glacés* and the chopped walnuts. Beat the eggs with a beater. Heat a low-sided frying-pan (preferably one in cast-iron) and when it is hot throw in a knob of butter. Pour in the eggs and raise the heat until they begin to set.

Put the cheese filling in the center of the omelette, fold it over and turn it carefully so that the other side may also get done.

Slide the omelette onto a serving dish, dust with sugar and decorate to taste with fresh or glacé fruit and dollops of jam.

$\frac{1}{2}$ cup mascarpone	2 eggs
(a rich full-fat cream cheese)	knob of butter
1 egg yolk	fresh or glacé fruit
1 tablespoon sugar	jam
1 tablespoon marrons glacés	
1 tablespoon shelled walnuts	

Moka Cake.

Winter

Tagliatelle Cake

Mix the flour with the egg yolks, the liqueur and enough vermouth to make the mixture medium thick. Work well, then roll out thinly. Leave the dough to dry, dust with flour, fold and cut into *tagliatelle*.

Mix together the sugar, cocoa, vanilla sugar, blanched, peeled and chopped almonds and pulverized macaroons.

Arrange a layer of *tagliatelle* in a buttered and floured cake pan, spread a layer of mixture over it, add another layer of *tagliatelle*, and so on until the pan is filled up. Dot the last layer with small pieces of butter and cook in a moderate oven for about 30 minutes.

1 lb flour	*$\frac{3}{4}$ cup cocoa*
4 egg yolks	*1 envelope vanilla sugar*
Sassuolo liqueur	*$\frac{1}{2}$ cup sweet almonds*
vermouth	*$\frac{1}{2}$ cup macaroons*
1 cup sugar	*$\frac{1}{2}$ cup butter*

Black Cherry Pie

Heap the flour and mix it with the sugar and the orange peel. Add 3 egg yolks, the softened butter and the white wine. Work lightly. Roll out and cut from the dough a round only an eighth of an inch high but large enough in diameter to line the bottom and sides of a buttered and floured pie plate. Fill the pie with plenty of jam and cover with thin strips of left-over dough in a criss-cross pattern. Brush the strips with beaten egg yolk and cook in a moderately warm oven for about 30 minutes. Decorate with black cherries and serve.

$2\frac{1}{2}$ cups flour	*$\frac{1}{2}$ cup butter*
$\frac{1}{2}$ cup sugar	*1 tablespoon white wine*
grated orange peel	*fruit jam for filling*
3 egg yolks	*black cherries for decoration*

Potato Pudding

Boil the potatoes and purée them. Heat them in a saucepan and mix in the butter, the cream, a pinch of salt and a spoonful of flour. Add the sugar, stirring all the time, a pinch of cinnamon, one of nutmeg, 3 egg yolks and, last, 3 stiffly beaten egg whites. Mix further, add the previously soaked raisins and the pine kernels and pour into a buttered and floured cake pan. Cook in a hot oven for about 45 minutes. Serve at once, sprinkled with powdered sugar.

1 lb. potatoes	*pinch of cinnamon*
½ cup butter	*pinch of nutmeg*
¾ cup cream	*3 eggs (separated)*
pinch of salt	*½ cup raisins*
tablespoonful of flour	*2 tablespoons pine kernels*
3 tablespoons sugar	*powdered sugar*

Saxon Pudding

Beat the butter in a saucepan until it is soft and frothy. Add the sugar and the flour and dilute with milk.
Cook, stirring all the time, first over moderate heat and then over a higher flame. When the mixture has thickened to the consistency of a paste, remove from heat. Add the egg yolks, then fold in carefully the stiffly beaten egg whites. Pour the mixture into a buttered and floured cake pan and cook in the oven in a *bain-marie*.
Serve hot, with *crème anglaise* or *zabaione* (pages 18 and 22).

½ cup butter	*5 eggs (separated)*
1 cup sugar	*crème anglaise or zabaione*
1 cup flour	
1¼ cups milk	

Kugelhupf

Mix vigorously in a bowl the butter, the sugar, the juice and grated peel of a lemon, until the mixture is white and frothy. Add the 3 egg yolks one by one and gradually the flour and a little milk, stirring all the time. Fold in 3 stiffly beaten egg whites, the soaked and floured raisins and, last, the yeast. Butter a metal bowl and sprinkle with breadcrumbs. Put the blanched and peeled almonds in the bottom and pour in the mixture. Cook in a moderate oven for 1 hour.

The Kugelhupf may be eaten fresh from the oven but it is preferable to let it cool properly first.

½ cup butter	a little milk
1 cup sugar	¼ cup raisins
1 lemon	1 envelope yeast
3 eggs (separated)	2 tablespoons almonds
1¾ cups flour	

Arianna Pudding

Add a pinch of vanilla to the milk and bring to the boil, then remove from heat. Beat the eggs with the sugar and add to the milk.

Butter a metal bowl and sprinkle it with sugar. Fill it with alternate layers of pieces of ladyfingers, sultanas and chopped glacé fruit soaked in rum. Then pour in the custard mixture little by little.

Cook in a *bain-marie* for at least 25 minutes, taking care that the water does not boil.

Allow to cool, then unmold onto a serving dish and cover with *zabaione* (see Basic Recipes section) mixed with a little whipped cream. Put a glacé fruit in the center of the cake, let it cool completely and serve.

2½ cups milk	½ cup glacé fruit
pinch of vanilla	1 small glass rum
3 tablespoons sugar	3-egg zabaione
3 eggs	whipped cream
generous ¼ lb ladyfingers	1 whole glacé fruit for decoration
½ cup sultanas	

Lemon Tart

Prepare some light sweet shortcrust pastry and some pastry cream according to the Basic Recipes and in the quantities given below.

Line a buttered and floured pie plate with the dough. Cover it with a sheet of wax paper weighed down with dried beans or peas to prevent the dough from rising.

Cook in a moderate oven for about 20 minutes, take out, remove the wax paper and the beans and allow to cool.

Spread the bottom of the tart with the pastry cream and fill up with the stiffly beaten egg whites sweetened with sugar and vanilla sugar. Sprinkle the surface with more sugar and cook in a moderate oven for 20 minutes.

For the shortcrust pastry	5 tablespoons sugar
1¾ cups flour	5 tablespoons flour
½ cup butter	2½ cups milk
½ cup sugar	grated lemon peel
2 egg yolks	For the meringue
salt	3 egg whites
½ teaspoon lemon peel (grated)	1 cup sugar
For the pastry cream	1 envelope vanilla sugar
4 egg yolks	

Opposite: Gâteau St Honoré

Arianna pudding

Sanguinaccio

First prepare the almonds: blanch, peel and chop them not too finely, then toast them in the oven for a few minutes.

In a small metal pot or saucepan, mix together the pig's blood, the milk, the sugar, the cocoa and the cinnamon. Heat over a low flame and stir continuously until the mixture begins to thicken. Then pour it into a bowl, sprinkle with the chopped almonds and chill.

2 tablespoons almonds	$\frac{3}{4}$ cup sugar
2$\frac{1}{2}$ cups pig's blood	$\frac{3}{4}$ cup cocoa
2$\frac{1}{2}$ cups milk	$\frac{1}{2}$ teaspoon powdered cinnamon

Apples Moscow

Choose six fine apples, preferably all the same size. Cut off the top without peeling them and scoop out most of the flesh.

Soak the apples in sweetened water for about 5 minutes. Remove them and put them top downwards on a plate so that they drain well.

Purée the scooped-out apple flesh, adding the flesh from the other two peeled and cored apples. Heat the purée, add a big knob of butter, two spoonfuls of sugar, a few spoonfuls of water and the juice of 1 lemon. When it is cooked add the apricot jam and, away from the heat, fold in the stiffly beaten egg whites.

Fill the apples with this mixture, put them on a buttered cookie sheet and cook in the oven for at least 10 minutes.

8 fine apples	1 lemon
knob of butter	1 cup apricot jam (sifted)
2$\frac{1}{2}$ tablespoons sugar	3 egg whites

Baked Bananas

Peel the bananas and make a deep incision lengthwise. Cream the butter and sugar vigorously together and put this in the incisions. Butter an ovenproof dish, pour in the water and a pinch of vanilla and arrange the bananas next to one another, sprinkling them with sugar. Cover with wax paper and cook in a moderate oven for at least 20 minutes.

6 thick, ripe bananas	2½ tablespoons water
2 tablespoons butter	pinch of vanilla
½ cup sugar	sugar to sprinkle

Moka Cake

The day before serving, prepare and cook some Genoese pastry according to the Basic Recipe, with the ingredients in the quantities given below.

Now make some *crème anglaise* (see Basic Recipes section). While this is cooling dot the bottom of a bowl with pieces of butter and pour in the lukewarm cream, stirring well until the mixture is smooth. Finally add the instant coffee, mixing a little more.

Cut the Genoese cake into three rounds. Spread the coffee cream very smoothly onto each of these with a knife moistened in hot water. Decorate with sliced almonds and allow to cool for at least 1 hour before serving.

For the pastry	For the filling and decoration
2¼ cups flour	1½ cups crème anglaise
1 cup sugar	1 cup butter
8 eggs	2½ tablespoons instant coffee
½ cup .butter	½ cup almonds

Gâteau St Honoré

Make the shortcrust and the choux pastry according to the Basic Recipes. Roll out the shortcrust pastry to a thin round about 8 in. in diameter. Put it on a buttered cookie sheet, and pipe a thin line of choux pastry all around the edge using a cloth pastry bag or pastry syringe with a plain funnel. Brush the whole surface of the pastry with the beaten egg, prick the bottom with a fork and cook in the oven for about 30 minutes. With the rest of the choux pastry in the pastry bag make small round *choux* the size of a thumbnail. Brush them with the beaten egg and cook in the oven for at least 15 minutes. Remove from heat and allow to cool.

Meanwhile dilute the sugar and honey with water in a saucepan. Heat and cook, stirring all the time over high heat until the sugar thickens and, when tasted, is no longer tacky.

Remove the mixture from the heat and with it moisten the bottom of the small *choux*, then arrange them around the edge of the cake. Allow to cool, then make a lateral incision in each *choux* and, by means of a small forcing bag, fill them with whipped cream.

Fill the centre of the cake with *crème St Honoré* (see page 20). The cake may also be decorated with glacé fruit.

½ *lb shortcrust pastry*	½ *tablespoon honey*
1 *lb choux pastry*	*whipped cream*
1 *beaten egg*	1½ *cups* crème St-Honoré
¾ *cup sugar*	

Almond Sweetmeats

Blanch the almonds in boiling water, peel them and slice them thinly. Make a thick syrup with the sugar and less than ½ a glass of water, add the orange-flower water, the sliced almonds and the grated lemon peel. After stirring thoroughly throw spoonfuls of the mixture onto a lightly oiled marble slab or wax paper.

Unstick the sweetmeats when they are cold.

1¼ *cups almonds*	*grated lemon peel*
2½ *cups sugar*	1 *small glass orange-flower water*

Fedora Cake

Soak the glacé cherries in some of the Kirsch.

Mix 2 of the eggs, the remaining Kirsch, the sugar and the powdered almonds together in a bowl. Work energetically for a few minutes and add the yolks of the remaining 3 eggs and the flour. Whip the egg whites until stiff and fold them delicately into the mixture. Add finally the melted and cooled butter and carry on mixing until it is blended with the rest.

Butter and flour a fairly high-sided cake pan. Pour in some of the mixture, arrange over it some of the Kirsch-flavored cherries, cover them with more of the mixture and so on until all the ingredients are used up. Cook in a moderate oven for about 40 minutes. Remove and allow to cool.

Reserve 12 of the biggest preserved cherries and chop up the rest finely. Mix them with the apricot jam (flavor with a few drops of *grappa* if liked). Cut the cake horizontally in two pieces and put the chopped up cherries in between, making sure the stuffing is not visible from the outside. Glaze the cake with a sugar-and-Kirsch glaze. Decorate the surface with chopped roasted almonds arranged in a circle or spiral and the 12 preserved cherries all around the edge.

½ cup glacé cherries	½ cup butter
1 small glass Kirsch	1 cup cherries preserved in alcohol
5 eggs	1 cup apricot jam
¾ cup sugar	1¼ cups sugar and Kirsch glaze
½ cup powdered almonds	a few toasted almonds
½ cup flour	

Apple tart.

Orange Tart

Make ¾ lb puff pastry according to the basic recipe. Roll it out thinly and line a pie plate with it. Cover with wax paper weighed down with dried peas or beans. Cook in a hot oven for about 30 minutes. Meanwhile peel the oranges, separate the quarters and remove the pith.

When the pastry is cooked remove from the oven and allow to cool. Reduce the apricot jam over heat. Arrange the orange quarters in concentric circles over the pastry base and spread the apricot jam over them. Dust with sugar. The tart may also be decorated to taste with glacé fruit.

¾ lb puff pastry	sugar
2 lb oranges	glacé fruit (optional)
apricot jam	

Apple Tart

Make ¾ lb shortcrust pastry according to the Basic Recipe. Roll out thinly and use to line a buttered pie plate; prick the bottom with a fork and spread apple preserve flavored with a pinch of vanilla over the pastry base.

Peel and core the apples and slice them thinly. Arrange the slices so that they overlap in concentric circles over the apple preserve.

Cook in a hot oven for about 30 minutes. Remove, dust with sugar and spread some warmed apricot jam over the apples.

¾ lb shortcrust pastry	2 apples
¾ lb apple preserve	sugar
pinch of vanilla	apricot jam

Apple Cake

Cream the butter with the sugar and salt. Add the eggs and, gradually, the milk; then, mixing all the time, add the vanilla, the grated lemon peel, the flour and the yeast.

Pour half the mixture into a buttered and floured cake pan. Arrange a layer of thinly sliced apples over this, cover with the remaining mixture and finish with another layer of apples.

Cook in a moderate oven for about 35 minutes.

This apple cake may be eaten at any time and served on any occasion.

½ cup butter	vanilla
1¼ cups sugar	grated peel of 1 lemon
1 teaspoon salt	1¼ lb flour
4 eggs	1 envelope yeast
1¼ cups milk	3 apples

Pear Tart

Prepare ¾ lb shortcrust pastry according to the Basic Recipe. Roll out thinly and use to line a buttered pie plate. Prick the bottom with a fork and spread the apple preserve over it.

Peel and core the pears and cut them in half. Soak them for a few minutes in a sugar syrup (see Basic Recipes section), diluted with the red wine and warmed. Arrange the pears over the apple preserve and cook the tart in the oven for about 30 minutes.

Remove, turn out and spread some grape jelly all over the surface of the tart.

¾ lb shortcrust pastry	sugar syrup
¾ lb apple preserve	1 glass red wine
4 pears	grape jelly

Dobos Cake

Beat the egg yolks in a bowl with the flour, half the ordinary sugar and the teaspoon of vanilla-flavored sugar, adding also a few drops of lemon juice and a spoonful of cold water. When the mixture becomes frothy fold in delicately the stiffly beaten egg whites flavored with 1½ tablespoons of the remaining sugar and the grated peel of ½ a lemon. Work well so that the mixture becomes smooth. Butter 4 medium-sized pie plates and pour into each a small quantity of the mixture. Cook in a hot oven for about 10 minutes. Remove and allow to cool. On 3 of the 4 rounds of pastry spread chocolate-flavored butter cream (see page 29). Arrange the pastry rounds on top of one another, reserving the unbuttered one.

Make a caramel (see Basic Recipes) with the remaining sugar and the juice of $\frac{1}{2}$ a lemon and while it is still hot pour over the unbuttered pastry round. Cut this in about 10 slices and arrange these over the cake so that the base of each rests on a little pyramid of butter cream.

8 eggs (separated)	1 lemon
$\frac{3}{4}$ lb sugar	1 cup chocolate butter cream
1 teaspoon vanilla sugar	$1\frac{1}{2}$ cups flour

Stollen Torte

Pour the flour into a bowl, make a well in the center and put in the sugar, the 2 whole eggs, the milk, the softened butter and a pinch of salt. Work until the mixture is soft and smooth, then add the chopped almonds and the sultanas. Flavor with rum and orange juice. Work the dough a little more, then shape it into a loaf.

Put the loaf onto a buttered and floured cookie sheet and brush the surface with melted butter (about $\frac{1}{2}$ tablespoon). Cook in a moderate oven for 15 minutes, then turn up the heat and cook for another 45 minutes.

When the cake is cooked pour a spoonful of sugar syrup (page 27) over it.

$2\frac{1}{2}$ cups flour	$\frac{1}{2}$ cup sultanas
3 tablespoons sugar	$1\frac{1}{2}$ tablespoons almonds
2 eggs	rum
$\frac{1}{2}$ cup milk	orange juice
1 cup butter	sugar syrup
pinch of salt	

Linz Torte

Make $\frac{3}{4}$ lb shortcrust pastry according to the Basic Recipe and add a pinch of cinnamon while working on the dough.

Roll out and use to line a buttered pie plate. Fill with raspberry jam, cover with strips of shortcrust pastry in a criss-cross pattern, brush with beaten egg and cook in a hot oven for at least 30 minutes.

$\frac{3}{4}$ lb short-crust pastry flavored	raspberry jam
with cinnamon	1 egg

Cream cake.

Below: Swiss flan.

Pumpkin Tart

Peel and clean the pumpkin, put it in a cloth and squeeze so as to remove excess water. If the recipe is followed to the letter 2 lb of pumpkin will be reduced to about 9½ oz. Soak the pumpkin in the milk and cook. Meanwhile pound the blanched and peeled almonds in a mortar with the sugar until they are reduced to powder. When the pumpkin is cooked add the pulverized almonds, the butter and the breadcrumbs, together with a pinch of salt. Allow to cool, then add the eggs and stir well.

Make a simple dough by mixing a little flour with some water and a pinch of salt. Knead well, roll out and use to line a buttered pie plate sprinkled with breadcrumbs. Fill up with the pumpkin mixture, cover with buttered paper and cook in a moderate oven. When the pastry is hard the pumpkin tart is ready. Remove the buttered paper, turn out and allow to stand a while before serving, for if the pumpkin tart tastes good when warm it tastes even better cold.

2 lb pumpkin	½ cup breadcrumbs
½ cup milk	pinch of salt
½ cup sweet almonds	3 eggs
½ cup sugar	flour (to make simple
1 tablespoon butter	flour and water dough)

Potato Cake

Boil the potatoes, peel and purée them. Blanch and peel the almonds and pound them with the sugar until they are reduced to powder. Add them to the potato purée, together with the melted butter, the grated lemon peel, a pinch of salt and the eggs, one at a time. Mix well and for a long time. Put the mixture into a buttered cake pan sprinkled with breadcrumbs and cook in a hot oven.

Serve cold.

1½ lb starchy potatoes	1 tablespoon butter
2½ tablespoons sweet almonds	grated lemon peel
a few bitter almonds	pinch of salt
¾ cup sugar	5 eggs

Swiss Flan

Make 1 lb shortcrust pastry according to the Basic Recipe. Allow to stand for 30 minutes, then roll out thinly. Use to line a buttered and floured pie plate.

Make the filling by mixing the flour with the cold milk, adding the butter, a pinch of salt and a pinch of grated nutmeg. Remove from the heat and, still stirring, fold in the grated cheese, the egg yolks and the stiffly beaten egg whites. Pour the filling into the pastry-lined plate and cook in a moderate oven for at least 20 minutes.

As is evident the Swiss flan is a cheese quiche without any sugar. Nevertheless it can be eaten as a savoury at the end of a meal, although it is perhaps better eaten as a main course.

1 lb shortcrust pastry	pinch of salt
$\frac{1}{2}$ cup flour	pinch of nutmeg
$2\frac{1}{2}$ cups milk	$\frac{3}{4}$ cup grated Emmenthal cheese
2 tablespoons butter	2 eggs (separated)

Cream Cake

Beat the sugar and the eggs together until thick, then add the flour and starch sifted together and the melted butter. Pour the mixture into a round buttered and floured cake pan and cook in a hot oven for at least 30 minutes. Remove and allow to cool. In the meantime whip up the cream and when the cake has cooled cut it in half horizontally and spread the cream in the middle. Dot the top of the cake with dollops of whipped cream. Dust with powdered sugar, decorate with cubed glacé fruit and chill well.

$\frac{3}{4}$ cup sugar	2 tablespoons butter
3 eggs	$2\frac{1}{2}$ cups cream
$1\frac{1}{2}$ cups flour	powdered sugar
$\frac{1}{2}$ cup starch	glacé fruit for decoration

Chestnut and Chocolate Cake

Drain the chestnuts, making sure they do not break. Put the syrup in a cup together with the Maraschino. Make two sponge cakes according to the Basic Recipe for Genoese pastry. Cut the sponge cakes horizontally into 4 slices. Moisten each layer with the Maraschino syrup.
Melt the chocolate in a double saucepan, remove from heat and add the floured and pounded almonds.

Opposite: Chestnut pudding with cream.

Lemon meringue pie.

Put a layer of sponge cake on a serving dish, spread a layer of chocolate cream over it; cover with a second round and spread with the chestnut purée, and so on. The last layer should be spread with chestnut purée and decorated with the chestnuts in the center, surrounded by glacé cherries.

1 can chestnuts in syrup	½ lb chocolate
1 cup Maraschino	2 tablespoons floured almonds
2 sponge cakes, about 6½–7 in. in diameter	1 jar chestnut purée
	¾ cup small glacé cherries

Lemon Meringue Pie

Mix together the flour, the butter, a pinch of salt and enough water to make a rather firm mixture. Roll out to a thickness of about $\frac{1}{4}$ in. Line a buttered and floured pie plate with this, cover with a sheet of wax paper weighed down with dried beans and cook in a hot oven for 10 minutes, then in a moderate oven for another 20 minutes.

Meanwhile prepare the filling: boil the water flavored with the grated lemon peel. Blend in a cup the flour with the lemon juice and add the water after it has boiled. Pour the whole thing into a saucepan and bring to the boil again, stirring carefully for 5–6 minutes.

Remove and add the sugar and egg yolks. Mix a little more and with this fill the baked pie base.

Make the meringue by beating stiffly 2 egg whites and adding sugar. Spread this over the filling and, if you wish, decorate with glacé cherries. Put again in a hot oven for a few minutes so that the meringue can turn golden. Remove and serve at once.

For the pastry	For the cream filling
$2\frac{1}{4}$ cups flour	$1\frac{1}{4}$ cups water
$\frac{1}{2}$ cup butter	peel and juice of 3 lemons
pinch of salt	$\frac{1}{2}$ cup flour
	$\frac{3}{4}$ cup sugar
For the meringue	3 egg yolks
2 egg whites	
$\frac{1}{2}$ cup sugar	
glacé cherries	

Verviers Cake

Put the flour in a bowl, make a well in the center and pour in the yeast diluted with $\frac{1}{2}$ cup of lukewarm milk. Mix well and for a long time, and allow to stand for a while. Then add the rest of the milk, the eggs, the butter, a pinch of vanilla and one of cinnamon. Blend the lot together, then cover with a cloth and allow to stand a little longer. Finally fold in the sugar carefully and pour the mixture into a buttered and floured cake pan. Brush the top with some egg white, allow to stand again for 30 minutes and finally cook in a moderate oven for about 1 hour.

1 lb flour	$\frac{1}{2}$ cup butter
$\frac{1}{2}$ packet yeast	pinch of vanilla
$1\frac{1}{4}$ cups milk	pinch of cinnamon
2 eggs	1 cup sugar

Apricot Omelette

Add a pinch of salt and a teaspoon of sugar to the eggs and beat vigorously. Melt the butter in a frying pan and when it is very hot put in the eggs. Put the apricot jam in the center of the omelette just before folding it over. When the omelette is ready put it on a serving dish and dust with powdered sugar.

4 eggs	*butter*
pinch of salt	*apricot jam (sifted)*
teaspoon of sugar	*powdered sugar*

Chestnut Pudding with Cream

Cook the chestnuts in slightly salted water, then peel them, clean them well and purée them. Add the sugar, the grated chocolate and the citron liqueur.
In the center of the dish place a saucer upside down and arrange the chestnut purée (previously sifted through a wide-meshed sifter) all round it. Even out with the fingers, remove the saucer and fill in the hole with whipped cream. Chill well before serving.

1 lb chestnuts	*$\frac{1}{2}$ cup chocolate*
pinch of salt	*$\frac{1}{2}$ cup citron liqueur*
$1\frac{1}{4}$ cups sugar	*whipped cream*

Chocolate Pudding

Put the milk and the grated chocolate into a saucepan, and heat. When it comes to the boil add the sugar and the crumbled ladyfingers.
Cook for 30 minutes, stirring every now and then, then remove from heat and put through a cloth.
When the mixture is cold add the beaten eggs and a pinch of vanilla and pour into a smooth cake pan caramelized with a little melted sugar. Cook in a *bain-marie*, unmold and serve chilled.

2 pints milk	*$\frac{1}{2}$ cup ladyfingers*
$\frac{1}{2}$ cup chocolate	*3 eggs*
3 tablespoons sugar	*pinch of vanilla*

Chocolate pudding can be dressed very lavishly.

Floating Islands

Boil the milk with a stick of vanilla. Beat the egg yolks with the sugar and add the hot milk a little at a time, stirring vigorously with a wooden spoon.

Pour into a saucepan and cook over moderate heat, stirring all the time, until the cream becomes thick and smooth. Remove from heat before it hardens, allow to cool and then chill.

In the meantime beat the egg whites until stiff and heat some water in a large saucepan; when the water boils slide spoonfuls of egg white into it; leave them in for two or three

154

Floating Islands.

seconds, turn them over and, after another few seconds, remove them. Drain them well and place them on absorbent paper. Continue this process until all the egg whites have been used up.

Just before serving remove the cream from the refrigerator, put it in a large bowl or in individual ones and arrange on top the whipped and poached egg whites.

2 pints milk	*6 eggs (separated)*
1 small stick vanilla	*½ cup sugar*

Sweet Polenta

Make a *polenta* by combining in a saucepan the flour with the milk and sugar. When the mixture is cooked, remove from heat, allow to cool a little, then add the whole egg and 4 yolks, the butter and the grated lemon peel. Mix well until the cream is smooth and divide it into two lots. Add the cocoa to one of these. Pour a layer of plain mixture into a buttered cake pan sprinkled with breadcrumbs, cover it completely with vanilla wafers, pour in a layer of cocoa-flavored mixture, and so on.
Cook in a moderate oven for about 20 minutes. Allow to cool and serve.

$\frac{3}{4}$ *cup flour*	*2 tablespoons butter*
1$\frac{1}{2}$ pints milk	*grated peel of 2 lemons*
$\frac{1}{2}$ *cup sugar*	*2 tablespoons sweet cocoa*
1 egg	*vanilla wafers*
4 extra egg yolks	

Rice Pudding with Almonds and Glacé Fruit

Chop the glacé fruit and put it in a bowl with the sultanas. Add some cognac and macerate. Bring the milk to the boil in a saucepan with the sugar and a pinch of vanilla sugar. When it starts to boil pour in the rice and 1$\frac{1}{2}$ tablespoons of butter and let it cook for about 20 minutes. Transfer the rice into a bowl, add 3 egg yolks, the cream, the macerated glacé fruit and sultana mixture. Mix well and fold in carefully the stiffly beaten egg whites. Pour this mixture into a buttered charlotte mold and cook in a *bain-marie* in the oven for about 20 minutes.
Remove from oven, allow to stand a little and unmould onto a serving dish.

2 tablespoons glacé fruit	*pinch of vanilla sugar*
2 tablespoons sultanas	*1 cup rice*
$\frac{1}{2}$ *small glass cognac*	*1$\frac{1}{2}$ tablespoons butter*
2 pints milk	*3 eggs (separated)*
$\frac{1}{2}$ *cup sugar*	*2$\frac{1}{2}$ tablespoons cream*

Sacher Torte

Beat the sugar with the eggs, then slowly add the flour and cocoa mixed together. Work energetically.

Pour the paste into a round buttered and floured cake pan and cook in the oven for at least 30 minutes. Turn out and allow to cool.

Cut the cake horizontally into 3 rounds. Soak 1 layer with rum. Spread one of the plain layers with jam, cover with the rum-soaked layer, spread this with a layer of jam, and finally cover it with the third layer.

Melt the chocolate in a double saucepan and pour it carefully over the cake so as to cover it completely. The cake may be decorated with sugar grains, etc.

1 cup sugar	*4 tablespoons raspberry jam*
6 eggs	*1 small glass rum*
2½ cups flour	*2½ cups chocolate icing*
2 tablespoons cocoa	

Pears in Red Wine

It is essential, to ensure the success of this recipe, that the pears should be of excellent quality and not too ripe.

Wash the pears carefully, dry them and put them in a high-sided saucepan. Sprinkle them with sugar, flavor with a pinch of cinnamon, the orange and lemon rind and a few cloves. Add the red wine and cook until the wine has evaporated.

6 pears	*orange and lemon peel*
3 cups sugar	*a few cloves*
pinch of cinnamon	*2½ cups red wine*

Marrons Glacés Dessert

Whip the cream. When it starts to thicken add the sifted fine sugar a little at a time and delicately.

Set aside some whole *marrons glacés*. Crumble the rest. Arrange the crumbled pieces in the bottom of individual dessert bowls, cover with the whipped cream and top each with a whole *marron glacé*. Sprinkle the cream with grains of colored sugar.

2½ cups chilled single cream	*¾ cup colored sugar for*
1 cup sugar	*decoration*
1¼ cups marrons glacés	

Sacher Torte.

Opposite: Pears in Red Wine.

Marrons Glacé Dessert.

SPECIAL OCCASIONS

Crèpes suzettes.

Opposite: above, Melon Bavarois.

Opposite: below, Royal cream baba.

Crêpes Suzettes

Mix the flour with the sugar and a pinch of salt. Add the eggs and dilute the mixture with the glass of cognac and the orange-flower water, the melted butter and the cold milk, stirring carefully and for a long time.

Heat a cast-iron frying pan about 6–7 in. in diameter and butter it lightly.

Put a ladleful of pancake batter into the pan, tilting it all over so that the mixture spreads evenly. Cook on a high flame for 1 minute then turn the *crêpe* over, tossing it if possible, so that it may cook on the other side. For the filling, mix the sugar lumps with 3 tablespoons softened butter. Allow them to stand for 20 minutes, then add the orange juice. At the table, in a proper pancake pan with a small burner underneath, caramelize lightly a spoonful of sugar with the thin slices of lemon and orange peel, then pour in gradually the orange juice and sugar mixture and bring to the boil.

Now place the *crêpes*, folded into four, in the pan, adding gradually a little orange butter and a little cognac and leave them in until they are hot enough to serve. The *crêpes* may also be sprinkled with a tablespoon of cognac and flambéed.

1 cup flour	*16 lumps of sugar—8 rubbed with*
2 tablespoons sugar	*orange peel and 8 with lemon*
pinch of salt	*3 tablespoons butter*
2 eggs	*juice of 4 oranges*
1 spoonful orange-flower water	*spoonful of sugar*
1 small glass cognac	*2 thin slices orange peel*
1½ tablespoons butter	*2 thin slices lemon peel*
1¼ cups milk	*liqueur and cognac*
butter for frying	*orange-flavored butter*

Royal Cream Baba

Mix the flour in a bowl with the yeast soaked in milk and the eggs and work manually for 10 minutes. Warm the butter until soft and sprinkle it over the dough. Cover with a cloth and allow to stand in a warmish place until it has absorbed the butter. Finally add the sugar and blend it in well.

Pour the mixture into a buttered ring-shaped cake pan and cook in a hot oven for about 45 minutes. Remove and allow the baba to cool. In a saucepan heat the rum and soak in the baba for a few minutes so that it is thoroughly moistened. Allow to cool, then brush with the apricot jelly which should have been boiled for a minute beforehand. Allow to dry naturally.

Prepare a plain water glaze with the sugar and a few tablespoons of water. Glaze the baba and place in a hot oven for 1 minute. Allow to cool and finally place on a serving dish. Decorate with Chantilly cream (see Basic Recipe) and with peaches in syrup in the center and all around the edge.

2¼ cups flour	2½ cups rum
½ packet baker's yeast	apricot jelly
2½ tablespoons milk	1 cup sugar
4 eggs	1¼ cups Chantilly cream
2 tablespoons butter	1 can peaches in syrup
1 tablespoon sugar	

Melon Bavarois

Moisten the sugar with water in a saucepan and boil for 5 minutes. Peel the melon and remove the pits, dice the pulp and put it through a vegetable mill. Pour the melon purée into the sugar syrup and boil for 5 minutes until a rather thick purée is obtained.

Meanwhile prepare the cream: soak the isinglass in a bowl of cold water and boil the milk, adding the lemon peel when it is removed from heat. In a saucepan work the egg yolks with the sugar for 10 minutes, then add the potato flour and the hot milk, a little at a time. Heat this in a *bain-marie*, but make sure the water in the bottom pan does not boil. Mix continuously for about 12 minutes until the mixture is thick, the froth has disappeared and the cream coats the spoon. Now add the squeezed isinglass and mix for a minute until it melts. Strain the cream mixture into the melon purée. Mix all together and allow to cool, stirring occasionally.

Whip the cream separately and as soon as it is ready fold it delicately into the mixture.

Dip a 2-pint mold in cold water and fill it with the mixture. Cover and chill for at least 3 hours. Just before serving dip the mold into hot water for a few seconds, unmold and garnish the *bavarois* with sweetened whipped cream and chopped pistachios.

1½ cups sugar	1 teaspoon potato flour
¾ lb ripe melon pulp	1¼ cups whipped cream
5 sheets isinglass	
1¼ cups milk	To garnish
peel of 1 lemon	¾ cup whipped cream
4 egg yolks	2½ tablespoons sugar
½ cup sugar	pistachios

Ladyfinger Mold with Zabaione

Soak the sultanas, then dry them well. Chop the glacé citron finely. Dip the ladyfingers lightly into the marsala and arrange them in layers in a buttered ring-shaped mold, sprinkling each layer with the sultanas and citron. Make a cream separately by beating 2 of the eggs with ¼ cup of sugar, flavoring them with a pinch of vanilla and finally diluting them with ¾ cup of milk. Without cooking this, pour it into the mold over the ladyfingers. Now cook in a *bain-marie* in the oven. Meanwhile make a *zabaione* with 2 eggs beaten with the remaining sugar and diluted with ½ cup of marsala, mixing energetically over heat.
When the ladyfinger mold is cooked, remove from oven. Unmold and fill the central cavity with the *zabaione*.
The ladyfinger mold, by virtue of its ingredients, may be good eaten hot; however it is much more delicious if eaten well chilled.

½ cup sultanas	4 eggs
1 tablespoon glacé citron	½ cup sugar
1 cup ladyfingers	pinch of vanilla
½ cup marsala	¾ cup milk

Roman Punch

Dilute $\frac{1}{2}$ lb of sugar in 1 pint of water, add a little grated lemon and orange peel and boil for 5–6 minutes. Remove from heat, add the orange and lemon juice, strain through a cloth and put in an ice-cream freezer. Remember to stir the mixture from time to time. Meanwhile boil the remaining sugar, flavored with vanilla, with $\frac{1}{2}$ cup of water; pour it into a bowl containing 2 stiffly beaten egg whites, and mix delicately so that the ingredients are well blended. Allow to cool, then remove the ice from the freezer, mix the two together thoroughly, add the rum and finally pour into a bowl and serve at once.

1 lb sugar	*vanilla*
2 oranges	*2 egg whites*
2 lemons	*1 small glass rum*

A new way of serving fruit salad.

Typical Sicilian sweets.

Cassata Siciliana

Sieve the *Ricotta*, then mix it with the sugar, working with a spoon until it is soft and frothy. Add the Maraschino, the roughly chopped chocolate and the cubed glacé fruit. Make a ⅓ lb sponge cake according to the Basic Recipe for Genoese Pastry. Cut it into slices and with these line the bottom and sides of a smooth and high-sided cake pan. Pour the mixture into the pan, smooth the surface with a knife and cover with more sponge slices. Chill well. Just before serving unmold and cover with vanilla-flavored sugar or with a sugar glaze (see Basic Recipes). Decorate with glacé fruit to taste.

1 lb Ricotta *cheese*	*⅓ lb sponge cake*
1¼ cups sugar	*vanilla-flavored sugar*
1 small glass Maraschino	*or sugar glaze*
¾ cup chocolate	
½ cup glacé fruit	

Champagne Fruit Salad

Make a fruit salad with as many fruits in season as possible. Pour over it a sugar syrup (see Basic Recipes) and dilute with a glass of champagne, or more, according to the amount of fruit salad. Chill well before serving.

fruit salad	*dry champagne*
sugar syrup	

Mont-Blanc

Peel the chestnuts and remove the inner peel carefully. Cook them in the milk flavored with cinnamon. When they are cooked sift·them immediately Mix the rum and fine sugar with the chestnut purée. Allow to cool, then arrange the mixture, shaped into a cone, onto a serving dish.
Beat the cream until thick and dot it about the chestnut purée to give an effect of snow. Dust with fine sugar and serve.

1¼ lb chestnuts	*rum*
2 pints milk	*1¾ cups sugar*
cinnamon	*2½ cups fresh cream*

Sorrento Walnut Pudding

Beat the sugar in a bowl, adding the egg yolks one by one as you beat. When the sugar has melted completely, add the starch, the flour and the Kirsch. Continue to beat until the mixture is completely smooth and well blended.
Heat the milk separately and as soon as it boils pour it into the mixture in the bowl, stirring vigorously. Put in a saucepan and heat, stirring all the time, over moderate heat. Make sure the mixture does not become too thick. After it has boiled two or three times remove from heat, continue to stir for a few minutes and allow to cool.
While this is cooling chop the walnuts finely and cream the butter with the sugar until it is smooth and creamy. Add the walnuts to the butter and this to the cooling mixture.
Line a pan with wax paper and pour in the mixture. Chill for at least 24 hours.

This walnut pudding should be decorated with half walnuts and served with a luke-warm chocolate cream. To make the chocolate cream, melt some finely chopped chocolate in a small double saucepan, add the coffee, raise the heat and, stirring all the time, blend them well together. Then add the sugar and, when this has been absorbed, the cream. When this is thick, remove from heat, allow to cool a little and, just before serving, add the butter.

For the cream	For the chocolate cream
1 cup sugar	$\frac{1}{4}$ lb baking chocolate
3 egg yolks	1 glass strong coffee
1 tablespoon potato starch	4 lumps sugar
1 tablespoon flour	1 tablespoon light cream
$2\frac{1}{2}$ tablespoons Kirsch	1 tablespoon butter
$\frac{3}{4}$ cup milk	
1 cup peeled walnut kernels	For decoration
$\frac{3}{4}$ cup butter	halved peeled walnuts
$\frac{1}{2}$ cup sugar	

Birthday Cake

Cream together with a spatula the butter and the sugar flavored with a pinch of vanilla, then add the eggs and egg yolks one at a time. While stirring slowly, sprinkle in the flour and starch, sift together with the yeast, and continue to work until the mixture is smooth and well blended.

Butter a cake pan and sprinkle it with finely chopped hazelnuts. Pour in the mixture and cook in a previously heated oven for 20 minutes on moderate heat.

Turn out when the cake is cold, dust with powdered sugar and decorate with the traditional candles.

$\frac{1}{2}$ cup butter	$1\frac{1}{4}$ cups flour
$\frac{1}{2}$ cup sugar	$1\frac{3}{4}$ packets starch
pinch of vanilla	1 envelope yeast (reconstituted)
2 eggs	a few hazelnuts
2 egg yolks	powdered sugar

Two variations on a Mont-Blanc.

Sorrento Walnut pudding.

Mother's Day Cake

Beat 3 eggs with the sugar, add the flour and starch sifted together, then a melted knob of butter and a pinch of vanilla.

Butter a round cake pan, sprinkle with almond flakes and fill with the mixture. Cook in a hot oven for 30 minutes.

Meanwhile prepare the filling: mix together the cream cheese, the sugar, the egg yolks and the baking chocolate flakes. Work thoroughly with a spatula.

When the cake is cooked remove from the oven and allow to cool. Then cut it horizontally into 2 layers. Soak these on the inner side with Curaçao and spread with the filling. Put the two layers together again, spread the surface with the remaining cream filling and sprinkle all over with milk chocolate flakes. Decorate with a flower.

3 eggs	*2 tablespoons sugar*
½ cup sugar	*2 egg yolks*
1 cup flour	*2 tablespoons cream cheese*
1¾ packets starch	*2 tablespoons baking chocolate flakes*
knob of butter	*1 small glass Curaçao*
pinch of vanilla	*2½ cups milk chocolate flakes*
almond flakes	

Torta San Remigio

First make the cream: work the cream cheese with the fine sugar vigorously and flavor it with a pinch of vanilla.

Then prepare the cake: beat together the eggs and the sugar and sprinkle in the sifted flour, then the barely melted butter.

Butter and flour two cake pans, one round and one rectangular, and pour half the mixture in each. Cook in a hot oven for 35 minutes. Then take out and allow to cool.

Turn out the cakes and cut the rectangular one into cubes ½ in. thick. Cut the round cake horizontally into 2 layers. Spread some of the cream cheese mixture on one of these, cover with the other and spread the remaining mixture over that, spreading it more thickly in the centre. Dot the cakes with the cubes dusted with powdered sugar.

¾ lb mascarpone	*10 eggs*
(a rich cream cheese)	*1 cup powdered sugar*
1¾ cups fine sugar	*1 lb flour*
pinch of vanilla	*½ cup butter*

Koulitch

Pound the roasted almonds in a mortar. Mix the flour, $\frac{3}{4}$ cup of the sugar, the butter and the pounded almonds. After a few minutes add, while still stirring, 7 egg whites.

Pour the mixture in a low-sided buttered and floured cake pan. Cook in the oven for at least 30 minutes.

Prepare separately some almond paste by pounding the remaining almonds in a mortar with the rest of the sugar, adding after a while 1 egg white and finally some Kirsch. Continue to work until the ingredients are well blended. When the cake has cooled, decorate it in a spiral design by means of a syringe or a pastry bag filled with almond paste. Put in the oven for a minute so that the decoration may dry, remove, sprinkle with a Kirsch-flavored sugar syrup (Basic Recipes) and the chopped glacé fruit, and finally cover with apricot jam.

1 lb flour	Kirsch
1¼ cups roasted almonds	½ cup sugar syrup flavored
1 cup sugar	with Kirsch
½ cup butter	1 tablespoon glacé fruit
8 egg whites	1 cup apricot jam
2 tablespoons almonds	

Rice Pudding

Wash the rice several times in cold water, then cook it with the milk in a saucepan. Take care that it does not boil. The rice is ready when all the milk has been absorbed. Add the butter, the sugar and the grated nutmeg to taste. Allow to cool, then add the whole eggs and blend in well, mixing vigorously.

Butter a metal bowl or baking dish, pour in the mixture and cook in a moderate oven for about 1½ hours. Unmold onto a serving dish and dust with sugar.

¾ cup short grain rice	nutmeg
2 pints milk	2 eggs
1 tablespoon butter	sugar
1 tablespoon sugar	

Birnebrot

The night before serving, soak the pears, the apples and the figs in lukewarm water. The next morning make some pastry: first dilute the yeast in lukewarm milk. Put the flour into a bowl, make a well in the center and put in a pinch of salt, the butter and the softened yeast. Work energetically, adding gradually enough cold milk to obtain a thick paste. Cover with a cloth and allow to stand for 2–3 hours.

Drain the soaked fruit and chop roughly into a bowl. Add the finely chopped walnuts and hazelnuts, the sugar, the grated lemon peel, the lemon juice and the orange peel in small pieces. Dust with cinnamon and nutmeg and sprinkle with the water in which the fruit has soaked.

Roll out the dough to a thickness of $\frac{1}{4}$ in. in a rectangular shape. Put the fruit mixture in the center, fold the dough over so that it looks like a large loaf. Place on a buttered cookie sheet, brush with egg yolk and cook in a hot oven for 40 minutes.

$\frac{3}{4}$ cup canned pears	2 tablespoons hazelnuts
$\frac{3}{4}$ cup canned apples	2 tablespoons walnuts
$\frac{3}{4}$ cup dried figs	$\frac{1}{2}$ cup sugar
$\frac{1}{2}$ packet baker's yeast	grated rind and juice of 1 lemon
milk	1 tablespoon candied orange peel
1 lb flour	cinnamon
pinch of salt	nutmeg
$1\frac{1}{2}$ tablespoons butter	

Mother's Day Cake.

Torta San Remigio.

Cashew Nut Tart.

Cashew Nut Tart

Make some light, sweet shortcrust pastry according to the Basic Recipe and roll it out to a thickness of about $\frac{1}{4}$ in. Line with this a buttered and floured pie plate right up to the edges. Mix the cashew nuts and the eggs and sugar into a paste, working energetically. Whip up the egg whites until stiff and fold them in delicately.

Fill the dough-lined pie plate with this and cook in a hot oven for at least 30 minutes.

$1\frac{1}{4}$ lb shortcrust pastry	$\frac{1}{2}$ cup sugar
$\frac{3}{4}$ lb unsalted cashew nuts	8 egg whites
6 eggs	

Apricot Pie

Mix the butter with half the sugar and the flour in a bowl and work well until the mixture is smooth and well blended. Add the chocolate, vanilla sugar, the egg yolks one at a time and finally the rest of the sugar. Finally whip up the egg whites until stiff and fold them in delicately.

Pour this into a buttered and floured pie plate and cook in a hot oven for about 30 minutes. Allow the pie to cool in the plate, then turn out and spread with warmed apricot jelly.

¾ cup butter	1 cup flour
1½ cups sugar	1 envelope vanilla sugar
1 cup grated chocolate	¾ cup apricot jelly
6 eggs (separated)	

Kranz Torte

Mix the eggs, the sugar and the softened butter in a bowl. Work energetically and for a long time, then add the flour and starch mixed together and the grated lemon peel.

Knead the paste until smooth and well blended and then add the sifted yeast. Pour this into a buttered and floured cake pan. Cook in the oven for about 35 minutes. Remove, allow to cool, then turn out. Slice the cake into 4, soak each slice with Kirsch and spread with butter whipped with vanilla.

Put the slices back together again, spread the outside of the cake with butter whipped with vanilla and sprinkle with the almond sweetmeats in small pieces. Decorate with dollops of butter cream and, if wished, with glacé fruit to taste.

3 eggs	½ teaspoon dried yeast, reconstituted
½ cup sugar	Kirsch
½ cup butter	1½ cups butter cream flavored
¾ cup flour	with vanilla
¾ cup starch	¾ cup almond sweetmeats
grated peel of 1 lemon	glacé fruit

FEAST DAYS AND FESTIVALS

New Year's Day

Ring Fritters

Mix the eggs, the sugar and the liqueur together in a bowl, flavoring with a pinch of vanilla and one of cinnamon. Stirring all the time, add gradually enough flour to make a dough similar to bread dough. Cut this into small pieces, roll them into fine fingers and shape them into rings.

Fry in boiling oil, and remove from the frying pan when only half done and make a horizontal incision in each. Then fry again until golden. Drain on absorbent paper and eat either hot or cold.

4 eggs	*cinnamon*
½ tablespoon sugar	*flour*
1 small glass liqueur	*olive oil for frying*
vanilla	

La Buonissima

Make some light, sweet shortcrust pastry according to the Basic Recipe. It should weigh about 2 lb 10 oz. Roll out two rounds about ¼ in. thick, one of which should have a slightly larger diameter than the other. Use this one to line a buttered and floured pie plate and reserve the second round as a cover.

Separately mix the peeled and chopped walnuts in a bowl with the honey and rum for about 10 minutes. Pour the mixture into the pie plate and cover with the remaining pastry round. Press the edges together with the fingers. Cook in a moderate oven for at least 40 minutes. Turn out when cold, cover with a sugar glaze and serve.

For the pastry	For the filling
1 lb flour	*1¼ cups shelled walnuts*
½ lb sugar	*1¼ cups honey*
½ lb butter	*2 tablespoons rum*
lemon peel	
5 eggs	
pinch of salt	*sugar glaze*

Epiphany

Millefeuilles

Make about $\frac{3}{4}$ lb puff pastry according to the Basic Recipe. Divide it into 4 and roll out each piece to a thickness of about $\frac{1}{4}$ in., making sure that the pieces all have the same shape. Butter lightly a cookie sheet, put the pieces of dough on it and prick each piece with a fork before cooking them in the oven.

The sheets of dough are ready when they start to color. Remove from the oven, allow to cool and place one sheet on a serving dish. Cover it with a layer of pastry cream (see the Basic Recipe), cover this with the second sheet and so on. The last sheet of dough should not be covered with cream but dusted with powdered sugar or, if preferred, glazed by means of a sugar glaze. The pastry cream may also be replaced by jam (or, better still, jelly) to taste; or else cream and jam may be used as alternate fillings.

$\frac{3}{4}$ *lb puff pastry*	*vanilla-flavored powdered sugar*
1 cup pastry cream	*or sugar glaze*

Semolina Fritters

Mix the semolina in a saucepan with the milk, sugar and grated lemon peel. Cook for 10 minutes; remove and add 3 eggs and a pinch of bicarbonate of soda, making sure that the eggs bind the mixture properly. Fry in boiling oil, a spoonful of the batter at a time.

1 cup semolina	*3 eggs*
2$\frac{1}{2}$ cups milk	*pinch of bicarbonate of soda*
2 tablespoons sugar	*oil for frying*
grated lemon peel	

A selection of cakes for special occasions.

Carnival Time

Cavallucci (Sienese "Honey" Cakes)

Melt the sugar with a glass of water over heat until it reaches the "thread" stage. Away from the heat add the flour, the walnuts in small pieces, the aniseed, the spices, the cinnamon and the chopped glacé orange. Roll out the mixture to a thickness of little more than $\frac{1}{3}$ in. and cut into small shapes.

Put the honey cakes onto a buttered and floured cookie sheet and cook in the oven for about 45 minutes. Make sure they do not brown too much.

1 cup sugar	*pinch powdered aniseed*
2 cups flour	*pinch spices and cinnamon*
1 cup shelled walnuts	*2 tablespoons glacé orange*

Sfrappole, Chiacchiere, Galani or Cenci (Carnival Sweetmeats)

Mix the flour with the sugar, the 3 egg yolks, the liqueur, the grated lemon peel, the butter (previously melted over heat) and a pinch of salt. Work well, adding gradually enough milk to obtain a rather thick mixture. Roll out very thin and cut into long and narrow rectangles.

Twist these and shape them into bows. Then fry them in oil without letting them get golden. Dust with plenty of powdered sugar and eat cold.

If the flour is reduced to $\frac{3}{4}$ lb and the other ingredients left as they are, you can make the special Trieste and Trento fritters which are more crumbly and crisper.

generous 1 lb flour	*2 tablespoons butter*
2 tablespoons sugar	*pinch of salt*
3 egg yolks	*milk*
2½ tablespoons brandy, aquavit or rum	*oil for frying*
grated lemon peel	*powdered sugar*

Carnival Fritters

In a saucepan mix the milk, an equal quantity of water, the vanilla-flavored sugar, the bicarbonate of soda, the butter, a little lemon peel, a few small sticks of cinnamon and a pinch of salt. Bring to the boil, stirring continuously. Take off the heat, remove the cinnamon and lemon peel, add the flour, stirring carefully, and cook again, still stirring, until the mixture detaches itself from the sides of the pan. Remove from heat, allow to cool a little and add 8 eggs and 2 egg yolks, blending them in carefully. Flavor with 1 small glass rum or cognac and work a little more.

Cover the paste with a cloth or some wax paper and allow to stand for at least 3–4 hours. Heat a high-sided frying pan full of oil. Throw in the mixture, a spoonful at a time. Be careful not to put in too many *tortelli* at once. When they have puffed out, remove and drain on absorbent paper. Keep warm. Before serving sprinkle with powdered sugar.

1 cup milk	*$\frac{3}{4}$ lb flour*
$\frac{1}{2}$ cup vanilla-flavored sugar	*8 eggs*
$2\frac{1}{2}$ teaspoons bicarbonate of soda	*2 egg yolks*
$\frac{3}{4}$ cup butter	*1 small glass rum or cognac*
a little lemon peel	*oil for frying*
cinnamon sticks	*powdered sugar*
pinch of salt	

Castagnole (Lent Fritters)

Break the egg in a bowl and add 1 spoonful of sugar and 1 of good olive oil. Flavor with the grated lemon peel and a pinch of salt. Mix until it is well blended and add gradually enough flour to obtain a fairly thick mixture. Work a little more, then pour spoonfuls of the paste into a frying pan containing plenty of boiling oil. The fritters should float in the liquid until they are all puffed up and golden. Drain on absorbent paper and serve, dusted with powdered sugar.

1 egg	*lemon peel*	*oil for frying*
1 tablespoon sugar	*salt*	*powdered sugar*
oil	*flour*	

Carnival Sweetmeats.

Spiral Fritters

Mix the flour and pinch of salt to a paste with the bread dough, adding gradually enough water to obtain a smooth and soft dough. Work for a long time, with two 20-minute breaks in between to allow the dough to rise. The whole thing should take about 2 hours. After this time put the dough in a bowl, add the eggs, beaten slightly with a fork, and the milk, flavored with *grappa* and a pinch of saffron. Blend together well and allow to rise in a warm place. When the dough has doubled in volume put it through a large pastry syringe or pastry bag and pipe it in spiral shapes into hot oil.

Let the fritters get golden on both sides then drain on absorbent paper. Eat dusted with powdered sugar.

1¼ lb flour	salt
5 oz bread dough	saffron
3 eggs	oil for frying
1¼ cups milk	powdered sugar
1 tablespoon grappa	

Columbine's Fritters

Put the butter in a saucepan with the water, the sugar and a pinch of salt. Bring to the boil. Remove from heat and add all the flour at once, mixing vigorously. Continue to cook while stirring until the mixture is smooth and well blended and comes away from the sides of the pan. Remove from heat, allow to cool a little, then add the eggs and work to obtain a perfectly smooth and soft mixture. Allow to stand for 1½ hours, then pour spoonfuls of the mixture into a high-sided frying pan full of boiling oil. Fry a few at a time and let them puff up and cook properly. Drain on absorbent paper and serve hot, dusted with powdered sugar.

½ cup butter	1¾ cups flour
1 cup water	6 eggs
1 teaspoon sugar	oil for frying
pinch of salt	powdered sugar

Jam Ravioli

Make some shortcrust pastry according to the Basic Recipe and in the quantities given below. Roll out to a thickness of ¼ in. Cut out large rounds 3 in. in diameter from the dough. Fill them with a heaped tablespoon of jam each, fold them over and close well with a fork. Put them on a buttered and floured cookie sheet, brush them with egg and cook in a hot oven. Serve hot or cold, dusted with powdered sugar.

2¼ cups flour	lemon peel
½ cup butter	pinch of salt
½ cup sugar	jam for filling
2 egg yolks	powdered sugar

Easter

Easter Eve Panettone

Mix ¾ lb of the flour with the yeast diluted in a little milk. Work a little, gradually adding remaining milk and shape into a loaf; cover with a cloth and allow to rise until the next day.

The next day add the remaining flour to the loaf, as well as 2 of the eggs, working the paste vigorously until it is thick. Cover once again and allow to rise for another 7–8 hours. Finally add the 4 eggs remaining, the soaked and dried raisins, the chopped glacé fruit, the butter, melted over heat, the aniseed seeds, the pine kernels and the 2 types of sugar as well as the grated lemon peel.

Knead all this together until all the ingredients are well blended and shape in form of *panettone*. It may be cooked perfectly if done in the proper paper form used by Italian pastry makers, which allows the loaf to rise vertically. Once in the form, it should be placed on a floured and buttered cookie sheet and cooked in a hot oven for at least 1 hour.

The *panettone* is ready when a toothpick planted in the middle is found upon removal to be dry and clean.

This *panettone*, like all other *panettoni*, should be served cold.

2 lb flour	¾ cup butter
1 tablespoon baker's yeast	pinch aniseed seeds
¾ cup milk	2 tablespoons pine kernels
6 eggs	1¾ cups sugar
2 tablespoons raisins	1 tablespoon vanilla sugar
2 tablespoons mixed glacé fruit	grated lemon peel

Resurrection Cake

Blanch and peel the almonds. Pound them in a mortar with the sugar and the chopped citron. Add, if necessary, a little milk to soften the mixture. Put the mixture in a saucepan, adding the remaining milk, the chopped chocolate and the grated lemon peel. Bring to the boil, stirring all the time carefully. Remove from heat, allow to cool a little and finally add the strained pig's blood, the breadcrumbs, the honey, the butter and grated nutmeg to taste. Blend well and heat again, stirring carefully. The mixture will be ready when a spoon can stand in the middle.

Separately make some shortcrust pastry according to the Basic Recipe and in the quantities given below. Roll out to a thickness of $\frac{1}{4}$ in. line with this a buttered and floured cake pan and fill with the mixture. Cook in a moderate oven for at least 2 hours.

This cake is better served the next day.

For the filling	$\frac{1}{2}$ cup honey
1 cup almonds	2 tablespoons butter
$\frac{1}{2}$ cup sugar	$\frac{1}{2}$-nutmeg
$\frac{1}{2}$ cup glacé citron	
2 pints milk	For the pastry
$\frac{3}{4}$ cup chocolate	$1\frac{3}{4}$ cups flour
grated lemon peel	$\frac{1}{2}$ cup butter
$1\frac{1}{4}$ cups pig's blood	$\frac{1}{2}$ cup sugar
1 cup breadcrumbs	2 egg yolks

Easter Rings

In a bowl whip 4 eggs and 1 egg yolk with the sugar flavored with a pinch of cinnamon. When the mixture is frothy add the melted butter, stirring all the time, and the grated lemon peel.

Add the mixture to the flour mixed with the yeast: if necessary during the kneading add some milk so that the result is a smooth and well blended dough. Work some more, divide the dough into small pieces and shape these into small rings. Poach the rings in boiling water, using a perforated ladle, then put them on a buttered and floured cookie sheet. Brush them with egg yolk, sprinkle them with pine kernels and cook in a hot oven for at least 30 minutes.

4 eggs	*lemon peel*
1 egg yolk	*1½ lb flour*
1¼ cups sugar	*2 envelopes yeast, reconstituted*
pinch of cinnamon	*½ cup milk*
1 cup butter	*2 tablespoons pine kernels*

Easter Cake

Dilute the bicarbonate of soda and the cream of tartar in lukewarm water and add to the sugar and flour, adding the shortening gradually in small pieces and then 4 eggs. Work vigorously until the mixture is smooth and well blended, then pour it into a buttered and floured cake pan. Cover, allow to rise for at least 30 minutes, then brush with the egg yolk and sprinkle evenly with colored sugar granules.

Cook in a hot oven for about 45 minutes. Like all such cakes this Easter cake is better eaten cold.

1 teaspoon bicarbonate of soda	*½ cup shortening*
1 teaspoon cream of tartar	*4 eggs*
1 cup sugar	*an extra egg yolk*
1 lb flour	*colored sugar granules*

Angel's Bun

Mix the yeast with 2 tablespoons of flour, and dilute in a little lukewarm water. Allow to rise for about 1 hour.

After that time mix the flour with the eggs, the shortening in small pieces, the grated orange and lemon peels, a pinch of salt and the yeast mixture.

Wheat cake.

Knead well for a long time until the dough is soft, then add the sugar. Put the mixture in a well buttered and floured cake pan. Allow to rise for about 4 hours then cook in a hot oven, turning down the heat to moderate after the first 15 minutes. It should take about 1 hour altogether.
Serve cold.

1 teaspoon baker's yeast	*grated lemon and orange peel*
$\frac{3}{4}$ lb flour	*pinch of salt*
3 eggs	*$\frac{1}{2}$ cup sugar*
1 tablespoon shortening	

Easter Nests

Mix the flour with the sugar, the eggs, the shortening, the vanilla sugar and the ammonia carbonate. During the kneading add gradually enough milk to make the paste soft but thick. After kneading well for a long time roll out to a thickness of about $\frac{1}{2}$ in. Cut the sheet of dough into varied shapes: doves, hearts, stars, leaves, etc. It is advisable to cut out paper patterns beforehand and to use these as templates.
Place the dough shapes onto a buttered and floured cookie sheet. Each shape should then be covered by $\frac{1}{2}$ hard-boiled egg which should be dipped in water first so as to adhere to the dough. Fix the eggs to the dough base by means of pieces of dough.
Brush the Easter Nests with beaten egg and cook in a very hot oven until they are golden. Remove carefully from the tray and serve cold.

$2\frac{1}{4}$ lb flour	*1 envelope vanilla sugar*
$1\frac{1}{4}$ cups sugar	*1 tablespoon ammonia carbonate*
4 eggs	*$2\frac{1}{2}$ cups milk*
$1\frac{1}{4}$ cups shortening	*hardboiled eggs to fill the "nests"*

Wheat Cake

Pour the wheat into a saucepan, cover with water and soak for at least 2 days. Then after that time has elapsed cook for 1 hour. Remove, drain, replace in the saucepan and add the milk, 2 small slices lemon peel, 1 tablespoon sugar and a pinch of salt and cinnamon.

Simmer until all the milk has been absorbed. Remove and allow to cool. Pour the wheat into a bowl, remove the slices of lemon peel and add the remaining sugar, the *Ricotta* passed through a sieve, the cubed glacé citron, the orange-flower water, the grated lemon peel and another pinch of cinnamon. Knead the paste, adding the egg yolks and when it is well blended fold in carefully the stiffly beaten egg whites.

Make separately some shortcrust pastry according to the Basic Recipe and in the quantities given below.

Roll out, and with part of the dough line the base and sides of a high-sided pan spread with a little melted lard (or, if that is not available, butter). Pour in the prepared mixture and make sure the surface is smooth. With the remaining dough make strips and use in a criss-cross pattern over the filling. Make sure the dough base and cover are joined together. Reinforce the edges with extra bits of dough and flatten them with a fork. Finally brush with a beaten egg and cook in a moderate oven for about 1 hour and 15 minutes.

Remove, allow to cool and serve.

For the filling	4 egg yolks
$1\frac{1}{4}$ cups wheat	3 egg whites
$1\frac{1}{2}$ cups milk	
lemon peel	For the pastry
1 cup sugar	$1\frac{3}{4}$ cups flour
pinch of salt	$\frac{1}{2}$ cup sugar
cinnamon	$\frac{1}{2}$ cup lard or butter
3 cups Ricotta *cheese*	2 egg yolks
$\frac{1}{2}$ cup glacé citron	salt
$\frac{1}{2}$ glass orange-flower water	

All Saints

Milk Pudding

Mix the milk with the sugar, flavor with a pinch of vanilla and boil for at least 1 hour, stirring from time to time. Remove from heat and allow to cool. Then add the egg yolks and the beaten egg whites.

Separately prepare the pastry with a little flour, water and a pinch of salt. Knead well, roll out and use to line a buttered cake pan, sprinkled with breadcrumbs. Fill with the mixture, cover with buttered wax paper and cook in a moderate oven.

Serve cold.

2 pints milk	*2 egg whites*
½ cup sugar	*flour*
pinch of vanilla	*pinch of salt*
8 egg yolks	

All Saints' Day Bread

First prepare the ingredients for the mixture. Blanch the almonds in water, peel and chop them; crush the macaroons to a powder and soak the sultanas in lukewarm water, then dry them properly.

Now mix the flour with the crushed macaroons, the sultanas and the almonds; add the dried figs cut into small pieces, the sugar, a pinch of cinnamon and a little yeast. Make into a paste, adding first the egg whites, then, gradually, enough white wine to obtain a thick enough dough. Knead for a while, then divide the dough into several small pieces, shaping these into little oblong rolls. Put some pieces of rice paper onto a buttered and floured cookie sheet. Put the rolls onto these and cook in a moderate oven until the rolls are dried even inside: this can be tested by breaking one. Eat sprinkled with powdered sugar but not before they have been allowed to stand at least 2 days.

½ cup almonds	pinch of cinnamon
1 lb macaroons	pinch dried yeast, reconstituted
½ cup sultanas	4 egg whites
2¼ cups flour	white wine
½ cup dried figs	rice paper
1¼ cups sugar	powdered sugar

Whipped cream and jam omelette.

Sammartina

To start with moisten the blanched, peeled and chopped almonds, the chopped walnuts and the soaked raisins with a little cooked must. Separately prepare some shortcrust pastry according to the Basic Recipe and in the quantities given below. When this is ready add the nut mixture and mix; pour into a buttered and floured cake pan; even out with the fingers and cook in the oven at a moderate temperature. When the cake is ready turn out and sprinkle generously with colored sugar confetti.

For the pastry	For the nut mixture
$1\frac{3}{4}$ cups flour	$\frac{3}{4}$ cup almonds
1 cup butter	$\frac{3}{4}$ cup shelled walnuts
1 cup sugar	$\frac{1}{2}$ cup raisins
5 eggs	cooked must
lemon	
pinch of salt	sugar confetti

Simple Wheat Cake

Cover the wheat with water in a saucepan, boil for 5 minutes, then turn off the heat, cover with a lid and allow to stand until the next day. When the lid is removed the grains of corn will have opened. Drain them and dry them on a cloth. Then, holding the cloth in such a way as to wrap the wheat grains completely in it, beat and shake until the wheat is reduced to flour. Sift the flour through a very fine-meshed sieve and put it in a saucepan with enough water to make the mixture fairly liquid. Cook for at least 30 minutes over moderate heat, stirring all the time. Remove from heat and add the *Ricotta* cheese and honey to taste.

wheat grains	Ricotta *cheese*	honey

Cooked Wheat

This is a delicious dish which is also extremely simple to make. The only ingredients are wheat and cooked wine. First of all soak the wheat for at least a day. Drain well and put into a saucepan, preferably of fireproof pottery. Cover with water once again and cook over moderate heat until it is tender and has swollen. Drain well and serve in a cup after diluting it with some cooked wine, prepared according to the recipe on page 30.

wheat	cooked wine

Christmas

Panettone

Heap the flour onto the rolling board. Melt the baker's yeast in a little lukewarm water and put it in the centre of the flour heap, together with the egg yolks and the sugar. Add a pinch of salt and work lightly together; the mixture should not be too smooth. Soften the butter over heat and add it to the paste, without working it too thoroughly; then add the sultanas, soaked in water and carefully dried, the roughly chopped candied citron and the grated lemon peel.

Shape the dough into a ball and place it in the *pirottino* (the special paper *panettone* form). Allow to rise in a warmish place. When the dough has doubled in volume brush it with the beaten egg yolk; make a cross-like incision on the top and cook in a heated oven over moderate heat for about 40 minutes. The *panettone* will probably not be as perfect as a ready-made one the first time you try it, but although it will probably not be much to look at its taste should be good.

$\frac{3}{4}$ lb flour	$\frac{1}{2}$ cup butter
1 teaspoon yeast	$\frac{1}{2}$ cup sultanas
5 egg yolks	$\frac{1}{2}$ cup glacé citron
3 tablespoons sugar	grated peel of $\frac{1}{2}$ lemon
pinch of salt	

Pandoro

Mix together in a bowl the yeast, one egg yolk, $\frac{1}{2}$ tablespoon of sugar and $\frac{1}{2}$ cup of flour, adding water if necessary to obtain a soft mixture. Cover and allow to rise in a warmish place for about 2 hours.

Mix $\frac{3}{4}$ cup of flour, $3\frac{1}{2}$ tablespoons of sugar, 1 tablespoon of butter softened over heat and

3 egg yolks. Add the leavened mixture and work together for a long time and with energy until the two mixtures are well blended. Allow to rise in a warmish place for 2 hours. Then add the remaining flour, 3 tablespoons of sugar, 1½ tablespoons of butter softened over heat, 1 whole egg and 3 yolks. After another long kneading, allow the dough to rise once again. Work once more, this time adding the cream, the grated lemon peel and a pinch of vanilla sugar.

Roll out in a square shape and place in the center of the dough the remaining butter, then fold over. Roll out again, fold the dough over 3 times, roll out, fold it over another 3 times and roll out again. Allow to stand for about 30 minutes and repeat the performance twice. Finally allow the dough to stand for another 30 minutes. Shape the dough back into a ball and put it into one or two of the characteristic *pandoro* molds, buttered and sprinkled with sugar. Stand these in a warmish place until the dough has risen to the edge of the molds.

Pandoro.

Now place the molds into a hot oven and let them cook for 40–45 minutes, but remember to lower the heat after the first 15 minutes.

Turn out at once and serve cold, dusted with vanilla-flavored sugar.

1 teaspoon baker's yeast	$\frac{1}{2}$ cup fresh cream
7 egg yolks and 1 whole egg	grated peel of 1 lemon
1 cup sugar	vanilla sugar
1$\frac{1}{2}$ lb flour	vanilla-flavored sugar
1 cup butter	

Christmas Roll

Mix 1 tablespoon flour with the yeast melted in lukewarm milk and allow the mixture to rise to double its volume. Add the flour, the sugar, the butter, 2 egg yolks, the grated lemon and orange peels and 1 small glass of rum. Work the dough for a long time until it is soft and supple; the success of this recipe depends mainly on this phase of the operation. Roll out the dough on a well-floured dish cloth in a rectangular shape, about the thickness of one finger. Spread it with stiffly beaten egg whites and put on top of that the filling of minced walnuts, sugar, cocoa and grated lemon and orange peels. Add the raisins soaked in milk and the pine kernels. Finally dot the whole thing with small pieces of butter. Roll over and arrange in a spiral in a cake pan. Allow to stand for 1–2 hours. Cook in a moderate oven.

For the dough	For the filling
1 lb flour	1 cup walnuts
3$\frac{1}{2}$ packets yeast	$\frac{1}{2}$ cup sugar
$\frac{1}{2}$ cup milk	1 teaspoon cocoa
$\frac{1}{2}$ cup sugar	grated lemon and orange peel
$\frac{1}{2}$ cup butter	1 cup raisins soaked in milk
2 eggs (separated)	$\frac{1}{2}$ cup pine kernels
grated lemon and orange peel	
1 small glass rum	$\frac{1}{2}$ cup butter

Zelten

In a bowl put the sultanas soaked in lukewarm water and dried, then the dates, the figs, the glacé orange and citron, finely chopped, and the walnuts and pine kernels cut into small pieces. Add the *grappa* and cognac, a pinch of cinnamon, one of salt, and finally the rye paste.

Work well and for a long time until the mixture is smooth and well blended. Cut the dough into several little rolls, long and narrow in shape, and decorate them with whole almonds and chopped glacé fruit.

Put the *zelten* onto a buttered and floured cookie sheet and cook in a very hot oven for at least 15 minutes. Remove, cover with honey and allow to cool.

1 lb sultanas	4 tablespoons cognac
½ lb dates	pinch of cinnamon
¾ cup dried figs	pinch of salt
¾ cup glacé orange	¼ lb rye paste*
¾ cup glacé citron	almonds for decoration
½ cup shelled walnuts	glacé fruit for decoration
½ cup pine kernels	honey
2 tablespoons grappa	

* The rye paste is not easy to find; it may be found, however, in bakeries specializing in rye bread.

Panforte

Chop finely the almonds, the hazelnuts, the glacé fruit and the dried figs; blanch and peel the walnuts and chop finely also. Put all these ingredients in a bowl, add the cocoa, half the cinnamon, the clove, white pepper, coriander and mace. Mix together thoroughly. Put the honey and confectioner's sugar together in a stainless steel saucepan; heat and stir until a drop of the mixture solidifies in contact with water. Remove from heat, add the chopped fruit mixture, and mix until well blended. Line a wide and low-sided pan with wafers; pour in the mixture and cover with more wafers. Cook in a moderate oven for about 30 minutes. Remove, allow to cool, unmold and dust with powdered sugar and the remaining cinnamon. Wait for at least another day before serving.

1 cup peeled almonds	1 tablespoon sweet cocoa
½ cup roasted hazelnuts	pinch powdered cinnamon
½ cup glacé citron	pinch powdered spices: clove,
½ cup glacé pumpkin	coriander, mace, white pepper
½ cup glacé melon rind	½ cup honey
½ cup dried figs	1 cup confectioner's sugar
½ cup shelled walnuts	vanilla wafers

Yellow Bread

Mix the flour with the sugar, the oil, the powdered spices and the salt. Add the baker's yeast diluted in a little water and make into a paste, working well and adding gradually 1½ cups water. After a while add the blanched, peeled and halved almonds, the chopped orange and citron peel, the pine kernels and the soaked sultanas.

Mix a little more and with energy until the mixture is well blended, then cover and allow to stand in a warmish place for at least 12 hours. After that time knead a little more, divide the dough into small pieces and shape these into round and oblong rolls. (It will be easier to work with floured hands.) Place the rolls onto a buttered and floured cookie sheet, brush them with a rather thick mixture of water and flour, and cook in a moderate oven until a knitting needle inserted in the middle of a roll shows that they are cooked. Serve cold and preferably with a sweet dessert wine.

2¼ cups flour	1¼ lb almonds
3 tablespoons sugar	1½ cups glacé orange peel
1 tablespoon olive oil	1½ cups glacé citron
½ tablespoon spices	1¼ cups pine kernels
1 teaspoon salt	1¼ lb sultanas
1 teaspoon baker's yeast	flour for paste

Struffoli.

Below: Typical Calabrian sweets.

Struffoli

Mix the flour with a tablespoon of sugar, the grated peel of $\frac{1}{2}$ a lemon and a pinch of salt. Then mix this into a paste with the eggs, the yolks and the lard in little pieces. When the paste is smooth and well blended roll it into cylindrical shapes of the thickness of a finger. Slice these at an angle into lots of little discs. Fry them in plenty of oil until golden and drain on absorbent paper.

When the *struffoli* are ready, pour the honey into a saucepan and heat until it is almost liquid. Remove from heat, add the grated orange peel, the glacé citron and glacé orange peel, both finely chopped, and finally the *struffoli*, mixing these delicately so that they do not break. Wait a little, then pour the mixture onto a serving dish and arrange it into the shape of a ring. While the sweet is still warm sprinkle with colored sugar granules. Serve after a few hours.

$1\frac{1}{4}$ lb flour	2 egg yolks
$\frac{1}{2}$ cup lard	$\frac{3}{4}$ cup honey
1 tablespoon sugar	grated peel of 3 oranges
grated peel of $\frac{1}{2}$ lemon	$\frac{1}{2}$ cup glacé orange peel
pinch of salt	$\frac{1}{2}$ cup glacé citron
8 eggs	colored sugar granules

Honeyed Gnocchi

Mix the flour to a paste with the oil, the wine, the orange peel and a pinch of cinnamon. The result should be quite a soft paste, about the same consistency as the paste for potato gnocchi. Proceed as for the latter: shape it into a roll 2 fingers maximum in diameter. Cut this into small pieces and grate, as with gnocchi.

Fry these large-sized gnocchi in plenty of boiling oil. While they are getting golden prepare the glaze: pour the honey and orange juice into a saucepan and bring to the boil, stirring all the time, until they are perfectly melted. Remove from heat and soak the gnocchi in the honey mixture. Transfer onto a serving dish and serve at once.

1 lb flour	grated peel and juice of 1 orange
$\frac{1}{2}$ cup olive oil	pinch of cinnamon
$1\frac{1}{4}$ cups muscat wine	$\frac{1}{2}$ cup honey

Rigatelli

Mix the flour with the roasted and chopped almonds, the sugar and the yeast melted in a little water; flavor with a pinch of cinnamon and a clove. Mix to a paste with some luke-warm water added gradually until the mixture is well blended and thick. Roll out to a thickness of about $\frac{1}{2}$ in. and cut out cookie shapes with the help of a metal form or a knife; decorate the surface of these cookies with a fork and arrange them on a buttered and floured cookie sheet. Cook in a hot oven until they are completely cooked.

1 lb flour	*1 teaspoon dried yeast*
2 tablespoons almonds	*pinch of cinnamon*
1 cup sugar	*1 clove*

Opposite: Cassata and other Sicilian sweets.

Below: Iced Christmas bell.

Christmas Pudding (Italian Style)

Dice the glacé fruit and chop the almonds; soak the sultanas; remove the skin from around the ox kidney. Chop the suet finely.

Mix the flour into a paste with the salt, the sugar, the spices, the fat from the kidney, the fruit, the lemon and orange juice and a little grated orange and lemon peel. Work for a few minutes, then allow to stand for 30 minutes. Now add the eggs, the cognac, the milk and the breadcrumbs. Mix energetically for a long time until the mixture is well blended. Then put in a cool place for 1 night so that it sets a little. Butter a large metal bowl (or 2 smaller ones), sprinkle with breadcrumbs and pour in the mixture which should reach up to about 1 in. from the top. Cover with wax paper and cook in a *bain-marie* for at least 4 hours. (It is essential that the pudding should cook for a long time.) When it is cooked allow to cool, then chill.

Before the Christmas pudding is served, it must be boiled for 1 hour. Then unmold it onto a hot dish and decorate with sugar lumps steeped in warmed rum and cognac. Just before serving set fire to the sugar lumps and serve flambéed.

1¼ cups glacé citron and orange	1 lemon
¾ cup peeled almonds	1 orange
1½ cups sultanas	4 eggs
1¼ lb ox kidney	½ cup cognac
2½ cups flour	½ cup milk
pinch of salt	2 cups breadcrumbs
1½ cups sugar	sugar lumps steeped in
1 teaspoon mixed spices: cinnamon, clove, ginger and nutmeg	rum and cognac

Bûche de Noël

This is the classic French Christmas dessert. It may be made with a number of pastries and an equal number of cream fillings. But what remains the same is its external appearance: as its name implies, the *bûche de Noël* should look like a log of wood, complete with the stumps of lateral branches. In the best examples the surface of the log is patterned to look like the bark of a tree and the stumps should show the section of the wood.

This is one of the simplest recipes for this dish which always creates a festive atmosphere when it is brought to the table.

Boil, peel and purée the chestnuts beforehand. Melt the chocolate and butter in a saucepan. Add the sugar and the chestnut purée. Mix well until the paste is well blended. Chill for some time so that it hardens. Remove from the refrigerator and shape into a log of wood with two lateral branch stumps. Chill again and smooth the surface before serving, by means of a knife dipped in warm water. Imitate the surface of a bark with the help of a fork.

Glaze the log with a sugar glaze and chill again for a few minutes before serving.

2 cups baking chocolate	*2¼ lb chestnuts*
1 cup butter	*1 cup sugar glaze*

Genoese Panettone

Mix on a pastry board the flour, the sugar, a good pinch of salt, the grated lemon peel, the sultanas soaked in water and well dried, the chopped glacé citron and the pine kernels. Heap the ingredients together, make a well in the center and pour in the melted butter, the egg mixed with marsala and the lemon juice.

Blend in the ingredients with the fingertips, then add gradually the yeast reconstituted with about $\frac{1}{2}$ a glass of milk. Continue to work, kneading well and long enough to obtain a smooth and supple dough. Put the dough in a buttered and floured cake pan, make a cross-shaped incision on the top, cover with a cloth and allow to stand in a warmish place. Cook in a moderate oven for about 1 hour. Serve only when it has cooled properly.

1 lb flour	*2 tablespoons glacé citron*
1 cup sugar	*$\frac{1}{2}$ cup butter*
1 envelope yeast	*1 egg*
salt	*$\frac{1}{2}$ glass marsala*
peel of 1 lemon	*2 teaspoons lemon juice*
$\frac{1}{2}$ cup sultanas	*$\frac{1}{2}$ glass milk*
2 tablespoons pine kernels	

Opposite: Christmas pudding.

Below: Genoese Panettone.

RECIPE INDEX

PHOTOGRAPHS

Archivio Mondadori: 71, 143, 206—Arie de Zanger: 195—Ballo: 210—Bouillaud: 171—Castaldi: 191, 199, 203, 207—Cozzi: VI di sovraccoperta, 90—Dal Gal: 39, 46, 58, 67, 83, 94, 103, 106, 110, 111, 114, 115, 118, 127, 130, 131, 138, 147, 158, 162, 174, 175, 186—De Biasi: 167—Del Grande: 178—Editions des Deux Coqs d'Or: 23, 42, 47, 74, 82, 87, 114, 130, 131, 134, 150, 155, 159, 170, 211—Frai: 19, 22, 50–51, 111, 139, 147, 154, 163, 166—Ginori: 34, 46—Haertter: 94—Jardin des Modes: 26—Kobel: 127—Lloyd O'Neil Pty. Ltd: 63, 79, 183—Lotti: 151—Marie Claire: 119—Panicucci: 98, 123, 202—Syndication International: 31.